THE VENETIAN GHETTO

THE VENETIAN GHETTO

Roberta Curiel

Bernard Dov Cooperman

Photographs by Graziano Arici

RIZZOLI
NEW YORK

Frontispiece Interior of the Scuola Grande Spagnola

ACKNOWLEDGEMENT

The publishers would like to thank the Hebrew Community of Venice
for their permission to photograph the synagogues and the
photographer, Graziano Arici, for his work.

This edition first published 1990 by
Rizzoli International Publications Inc.,
300 Park Avenue South
New York,
NY 10010

Introduction copyright © 1990 Bernard Dov Cooperman
Text copyright © 1990 Arsenale Editrice
Photographs copyright © Graziano Arici
Translation © 1990 John Calmann and King

An Arsenale Editrice book

Library of Congress Cataloging-in-Publication Data
Cooperman, Bernard Dov, 1946–
    The Venetian Ghetto/Bernard Cooperman and Roberta Curiel.
    p. cm.
    Includes bibliographical references.
    ISBN 0–8478–1236–7
    1. Jews—Italy—Venice—Social life and customs.   2. Jews—Italy—
Venice—Pictorial works.   3. Venice (Italy)—Ethnic relations.
4. Venice (Italy)—Description—Views.   5. Synagogues—Italy—
Venice—Pictorial works.   I. Curiel, Roberta.   II. Title.
DS135.I85V4232   1990
945.31004924—dc20   90–31505
                                                              CIP

This book was designed and produced by
John Calmann and King Ltd, London and Arsenale Editrice, Venice

Designed by Karen Stafford
Typeset by Wyvern Typesetting Ltd, Bristol
Printed in Italy by EBS, Verona

Contents

THE CREATION OF THE VENETIAN GHETTO

AN INTRODUCTION

Bernard Dov Cooperman

I stood in Venice,
on the Bridge of Sighs,
A palace and a prison on each hand.

— Lord Byron,
'Childe Harold's Pilgrimage',
c. IV, st. 1.

In the Ghetto Vecchio, near the bridge joining it to the Ghetto Nuovo, is the present-day rabbi's house. The same building contains the Renato Maestro Library, and the social centre of the Jewish Community of Venice.

What is a 'ghetto'? Nowadays, in English at least, the word describes any urban slum and its economically and racially undesirable inhabitants. The Nazis added their own horrifying layer of meaning to the word: the ghettos they created to enclose the Jews of central and eastern Europe were really way stations on the road to extermination. In the Jewish collective memory, the ghetto has become the quintessential symbol of a time when Jews lived as strangers separated from an implacably hostile society. It is hard to associate the quiet streets of the Venetian ghetto with such brutal memories. Could the beautiful city of San Marco with its canals and towers, its churches and art – could this city have created the most famous ghetto in history, indeed, have given the institution its very name? Although folk etymologists and modern scholars have suggested alternate, often quite ingenious, derivations for the word, it is generally accepted that the word 'ghetto' derives from Venice which in 1516 required Jews to live in an enclosed area once occupied by the *ghetto nuovo* or 'new foundry'.

Like the floating city in which it nestles, the Ghetto of Venice presents the visitor with a paradox. On the one hand, it is a symbol of oppression. The Ghetto's high walls starkly delimit the narrow confines and sombre isolation of Venetian Jewry. We can imagine the two gates closed and locked each night at midnight. We can picture the guards, maintained at Jewish expense, whose task was to ensure that no Jew dared to leave the Ghetto to walk the city's streets before the *Marnagona* bell announced morning from St. Mark's tower. But ironically the walls of the Ghetto represent tolerance as well – albeit a limited sort of tolerance not much in keeping with modern taste. For when the Ghetto of Venice was first established in 1516, most of western Europe had expelled its Jews altogether. England in 1290, France in 1306, Spain in 1492 and, through a forced conversion, Portugal in 1497 had all achieved Christian homogeneity by expelling the Jews. Venice herself had traditionally been loath to admit Jewish residents; her patriarch and priests had carefully protected the faithful from the contamination of Jewish infidelity, while her patrician merchants had jealously guarded the Rialto market from potential Jewish competition. Seen in historical context, therefore, the Ghetto was a social mechanism which allowed for the *admission* of Jews when older rationales no longer sufficed and when earlier arrangements had given way before strident demands for religious purity. The Venetian Ghetto was created at the point of tenuous equilibrium between two opposing forces: it was, at one and the same time, an entry way for Jews into Venice and an enclosure to keep them out.

The Ghetto in a sense belonged to the Jews though they could own none of its buildings. Its high walls offered both physical protection and social distance from an alien outside. The Ghetto's Jews did not refer to their enforced residence as a jail. Rather, it was the biblical 'camp of the Hebrews', a place of holiness while en route to the Promised Land. In Verona they declared a public celebration of its establishment. For the puritanical young rabbi, Samuel Aboab, who had first seen Venice as a 13-year-old student, the city's Ghetto seemed Isaiah's Jerusalem, and he

therefore objected vigorously to a proposed public theatre in the Ghetto lest the 'faithful city become a whore' (*Responsa Dvar Schmuel* (Venice: 1701/02) No. 4, f. 2ª). Aboab's attitude tells us much about Venetian Jewry's intense efforts to order their enclosed world; his choice of words tells us even more about how these Jews identified with their community-behind-walls and gloried in it.

In isolating the Jews within a separate quarter the Venetians were following old precedents. Since medieval times, Jews in many parts of Europe had requested, and been gran-

ted, separate streets or quarters. In some places these areas had been walled off, but this was a defensive rather than an exclusionary arrangement and it was the Jews themselves who had controlled entry into their area. By the twelfth century, however, the nature of these Jewish quarters had begun to change as western Christendom became more insistent on enforcing the social segregation of infidel Jews. Thus, in 1179, the Third Lateran Council declared that Jews could not employ Christian domestics in their homes nor, for that matter, could Christians live in the same building

Perspective map of Venice showing the Ghetto (centre), Jacopo de Barbari, 1500. Museo Civico Correr, Venice.

with Jews. By 1462 Frankfurt had forced its Jews to leave their centrally located homes and settle in a walled quarter on the outskirts of the city.

The merchants of Venice had a second medieval model for their Ghetto, one they had encountered when trading in the Byzantine east. The Jewish quarters in cities such as Constantinople were constitutionally more akin to merchants' compounds than to the ghettos that would emerge later in the west. Ironically, Jews would sometimes even share a walled compound with the Venetians who, for all their military and economic might, frequently needed day-to-day protection from the local populace. Throughout the Mediterranean region, it was quite customary for foreign merchants to be housed in a separate quarter; sometimes it was only a compound or *fondaco* – a combination warehouse and residential facility which might or might not be closed at night. The significant point is that in the east the social isolation of the Jews was not unique. When we try to evaluate the Venetian Ghetto, we must remember that sixteenth-century Venice also restricted the living quarters of Turkish and German merchants.

In Venice, perhaps more than anywhere else, the Ghetto drew consistently on both these models, the one based on religious principle and the other based on xenophobia and commercial rivalry. The Venetian Ghetto always served both religious sensibilities and commercial needs. It allowed Venice to maintain its religious purity while reacting to changed economic conditions.

The English poet Shelley's impression of Venice as 'a peopled labyrinth of walls' is quite appropriate to the Jewish experience in the city ('Lines written amongst the Euganean Hills' (1818), l. 90). Medieval Venice was expert at erecting walls to keep Jews out. It was not that the city fathers were unwilling to take advantage of Jewish services. Jewish moneylenders began serving the needs of the poor in Venice at roughly the same time as elsewhere in central and northern Italy – that is from the late thirteenth century. But whereas in most places the Jewish bankers were able to negotiate liberal residence privileges, in Venice these undesirables were kept as far away as possible. With the exception of a brief experimental period at the end of the fourteenth century, the Jews were consistently required to live in Mestre on the mainland, and a series of regulations restricted the number of days each Jew might annually spend in the city. There is some scholarly debate whether the island known as the 'Giudecca' derived its name from having once housed a Jewish community, or whether the name was a corruption of the dialect term 'Zudegà' from 'del giudicato' – the island assigned 'by the judges' and town council. One way or the other, any medieval Venetian Jewish community would have been small and transient.

The Jewish communities which soon emerged in Mestre and the nearby towns of the Venetian *terrafirma* drew their membership from many sources. From the south came the Italiani Jews claiming proud descent from those Judean nobles whom Titus had brought to Italy in chains after the conquest of Jerusalem in 70 C.E. Their traditions of wealth and learning, first developed under Byzantine and Muslim rule, had come to full flower in the Rome of the high middle ages where individual Jews had provided medical and financial services to the growing papal court. Gradually these Jews spread a closely woven network of entrepreneurial and familial ties to the towns lying north and east of Rome. In each town or region they negotiated a *condotta* or charter under which they contracted to establish a loanbank, to fund it at a certain level, and to extend loans to local citizens at favourable rates for a fixed number of years. In return, they were guaranteed banking rights and residential privileges for the life of the *condotta*, they were exempted from wearing the demeaning Jew badge, they were allowed to establish a synagogue and sometimes even a cemetery, and they were licensed to bring along a substantial number of retainers to work in their bank, serve in their household, ritually prepare their meat, teach their children and so on. Each small Jewish community became, effectively, a court centred on the banker himself whose control was absolute. And, as befitted their status, many of the wealthy bankers played the role of Mæcenas, patronizing Jewish scholars and poets on the model of contemporary Christian rulers and merchant princes. The irrepressible poetry of Dante's younger contemporary, Immanuel of Rome, captures well the affluence and breeding of these households, their Purim feasts enlivened by poetic contests in which lyric creativity was inspired by models from Italian literature and spiced with equal measures of biblical exegesis, Talmudic learning and philosophical analysis.

More numerous than the Italiani were the Tedeschi or Ashkenazi Jews from the German-speaking lands north of the Alps. The legal position

A banker in his private bank. From G. Grevembroch, *The Customs of the Venetians*, Museo Civico Correr, Venice.

of Jews in central Europe had been deteriorating steadily since the time of the First Crusade, and in the general panic which accompanied the first onslaught of the Black Death (1348–49) the Jews had often been massacred as 'well-poisoners'. Over the years, many had sought refuge to the south, carrying with them their own language (Yiddish) and religious rituals, their own traditions of Talmudic learning and, of course, their extensive experience as moneylenders. The same factors which had allowed the Italiani Jews to prosper also benefited the Ashkenazi loanbankers who established themselves throughout northeast Italy, in Istria, Friuli and throughout the various provinces under Venetian control.

Finally, we should mention the leavening of French and Provençal Jews which continued to flow into the region as a consequence of a series of partial expulsions from the fourteenth

The innumerable windows of the tenement blocks accentuate their unusual height. The restoration work being carried out at present will make these old dwellings more comfortable.

century onwards. Never numerous enough, at least in this part of Italy, to form separate communities, these Jews nevertheless added their own distinctive contribution to the cultural melting pot that was Renaissance Jewish life in Venice. Some would become loanbankers in their own right, while others would serve as physicians, rabbis, tutors and scribes to established Jewish families. The family of Leon da Modena seems to have been typical. In his diary (begun in 1617 or 1618), this colourful Venetian rabbi recorded the tradition that his father's family, of French origin, had maintained loanbanks in Modena, Bologna, and finally in two villages in the Veneto – Cologna and Montagnana. The family could also boast of prominent scholars including Leon's grandfather, an uncle and at least one of his first cousins.

These then were the loanbankers who gradually established themselves in Mestre and its environs, attracted above all by the opportunity to share, in however restricted a fashion, in the prosperity of Venice. Theirs was one of the most lucrative credit markets in the world. True, from the end of the fifteenth century, they had to compete with the Franciscan inspired public loan funds, the *Monti di Pietà*, but these latter proved incapable of completely replacing the Jewish banks, and the two types of credit institution often existed side by side in the same town. In the capital, moreover, no such *Monte* was ever introduced, and the Jews therefore remained the primary source of consumer credit and small loans.

And now circumstances contrived to move the Jews in from the periphery and to create the Venetian Ghetto. With the outbreak of the War of the League of Cambrai (1509),

hundreds of the Jews from Mestre, Padua and possibly elsewhere on the mainland sought refuge in the capital. There was an immediate danger that enemy soldiers would loot the banks that the Jews had left behind and steal huge quantities of what was, after all, Christian property. Moreover, the war made the huge tax payments which could be wrung from Jewish bankers especially important, and the city's population was more in need of the Jews' financial services than ever. The Venetian Senate had little choice but to condone the Jews' transfer into the city and even to allow the re-establishment of the Jewish banks there. The Jews were back in Venice, this time to stay.

But it was not easy for the Venetians to live with the results of their self-interested generosity. There was, first of all, the ambivalent legacy of a centuries-old religious tradition: while clear precedent allowed the state to admit Jews and to encourage their economic activities, canon law also argued for the restriction and segregation of these 'sworn enemies of Christ'. The Renaissance city, moreover, was a place in which social roles and social spaces were clearly demarcated. Differences of dress were often dictated not just by laws of fashion and affordability but by the laws of the state as well. The Jews would therefore have to be clearly marked as a separate caste. One year, therefore, Lenten penitence required that the Jews' hat would henceforth be yellow rather than black. The next year, Jewish physicians were forbidden to wear the wide 'ducal' sleeves which were the customary mark of their profession. But, most important, it was suggested that the Jews be forced to move into a separate quarter

A wooden bridge, which joins the little island of the Ghetto Nuovo to the Parrocchia di San Marcuola, leads via the *sotòportego* into the Ghetto.

of the city, the island site of the 'new foundry' or *ghetto nuovo*, a fortress-like block of apartments with only a single gate which might be locked at night. Despite the Jews' objections, the Senate seized upon the idea and, on 29 March 1516 the Jews were ordered to move into the Ghetto at rents, it should be added, one-third higher than those previously prevailing. In the coming years, each time the Jews' *condotta* came up for renewal there would be some who urged that they simply be expelled. But for most, the Ghetto was a sufficient divider, and the Jews were able to live within its walls for almost three hundred years.

Soon another group of Jews began making their way into the closed world of the Ghetto. These were Levantines (Levant meaning 'the east'), merchants who brought the spices, raw silk, hides and currants of the east to the quays of Venice and who

The Ghetto Nuovo was always the liveliest and most animated area in the Jewish quarter, and was the area most frequented by non-Jews.

A Levantine Jew. From G. Grevembroch, *The Customs of the Venetians*, Museo Civico Correr, Venice.

scoured that city's markets for European manufactures which they could send back to their eager customers in the Ottoman Empire in the east. Already centuries before, the spread of Venetian military and economic power in the east had brought the Jewish merchants of the Mediterranean islands, of the Greek peninsula and of Constantinople itself within the Venetian trading orbit. The *Serenissima* had even granted some of these Jews Venetian citizenship – albeit at the colonial level. Repeated efforts to restrict the trade of these merchants to the outlying territories had proven ultimately futile: when they could not ignore the laws altogether, the Jews had simply traded with the city through Venetian Christian 'frontmen'.

But the question of admitting Levantine Jewish traders in the sixteenth century was of quite a different order. Venice was no longer dominant in the eastern Mediterranean and if her own merchants were to have access to Ottoman ports, she would have to grant reciprocal privileges to Ottoman merchants in the west. Since, moreover, fewer and fewer young Venetians were these days willing to undergo the risks and hardships of travel to the east, the admission of Levantines became all the more attractive: at least the quays of Venice could thus maintain their traditional entrepôt function as a key centre of international trade. Venice had little choice but to follow the example of other Italian states and welcome Ottoman subjects to her port, and by 1524 legislation referred to the trading rights of Levantines in Venice as quite 'customary'. While Armenian, Greek Orthodox and even Turkish merchants took advantage of this opportunity, recent research has shown that

Jews were often the primary beneficiaries of the new policy.

Why Ottoman Jewry was in a special position to take advantage of these new trading opportunities is a complicated matter that need not concern us here. But there can be no doubt that many westerners had come to believe in the wealth and power of the eastern Jews. Rumour had it that the Jews exiled from Spain were now selling Europe's military secrets to the Turks, and that Jewish merchants formed a huge international spy network, intentionally spreading the plague in Europe. The issue was not just whether individual western-educated Jews had gained influence at the Sublime Porte and might be of benefit to Venice – although the Senate was not above using such Jews as representatives in the labyrinthine world of Turkish diplomacy or even quietly suggesting to the Sultan's Jewish doctor that the Ottoman ruler's death would be amply rewarded. Beyond any such immediate considerations, the success of the Jews in the Levant put the lie to one of the underlying historical assumptions upon which western policy towards Jews had been based. It was simply not true that God would punish those states which tolerated the infidel Jews in order to take advantage of their financial services. As the Cavalier Gabriele Moro pointed out in the 1519 Senate debate over tolerating Jews in Venice:

> The Jews were driven from Spain and exported great wealth therefrom. They then went to Constantinople and the Sultan Selim conquered both Syria and Egypt.
> (Quoted in B. Pullan, *Rich and Poor in Renaissance Venice*, 1971)

Such remarks reflect well the contemporary western mood of fear and self-doubt as Europeans realized that their cities were no longer safe from Turkish armies and that their ships no longer ruled the inland sea. But the exaggerated role assigned to Jews in explaining European decline and Ottoman success also reflects well the changed perception of the Jews. Jews were no longer merely moneylenders. They were also important merchants and power brokers in the east whose commerce was to be courted and whose influence was to be humbly sought. This is why the Jews figure so prominently among the eastern merchants who come to trade in Venice.

Venice resisted legitimizing the new Jewish role as long as she could. At first, the Levantines, legally termed *viandanti* or travelling merchants, were admitted for only brief stays; after concluding their business in the city they were obliged to leave and return home. During their visits, the Levantines may have initially shared quarters in a *fondaco* with Turks and other foreigners, but after 1516 they were able to rent facilities in the *ghetto nuovo*. But soon this arrangement proved insufficient. Venetian dependency on the Levantines had continued to grow until, by 1541, the city's Board of Trade noted that these Jews controlled 'the greater part of the merchandise which comes from upper and lower Romania [the European part of the former Byzantine Empire]'. As part of a general move to foster trade, therefore, the Board urged that the Levantines be given additional space, if necessary by allocating to them the 'old foundry' or *ghetto vecchio* which was adjacent to the present Jewish quarter. This new facility was meant as a *fondaco* and not as a per-

manent residence for the Jews. The latter were still forbidden to bring their families with them to Venice, and each was officially required to leave the city after a fixed period of time – initially four months, then two years and then, from 1549, one year.

There is considerable evidence that at least some of the Levantine merchants were able to evade these restrictions and establish *de facto* residence in Venice, even bringing their wives and children with them. If the vociferous objections of many among the Venetian *gentilezza* are any indication, the Jews had soon carved out an important role in the Venetian world business. By international treaty they could now demand passage for themselves and their goods on Venetian ships and thus overcome one of the Venetian merchants' most important commercial advantages. A complex trading network soon connected Jews in Salonika and Istanbul with their co-religionists in Venice who were commissioned for three to five years at a time to act as buying and selling agents. The Venetian authorities were well aware of the increasing value of Jewish trade and renewed the Levantines' trading licence every two years without fail.

Inevitably, the Levantines began to organize themselves into a community of sorts. Lacking a formal consul on a par with other merchant colonies, they turned to one of the more prominent and influential members of their group to represent them before the Venetian authorities. Hayim ben Saruk negotiated a tariff reduction on their behalf in 1571. In return the merchants promised to pay him fifty per cent of any profits which accrued over the coming ten years from his actions. Ben

Jewish oath-taking. From G. Grevembroch, *The Customs of the Venetians*, Museo Civico Correr, Venice.

The Scrolls of the Torah, written on parchment by hand with special ink, may not contain any errors, blots, or corrections. The task of writing and restoring was entrusted to special scribes. In Venice it was the responsibility of the Chief Rabbi of the community.

Saruk's representation of the community was still *ad hoc* and 'entrepreneurial'. Because the community had no formal powers of enforcement, Ben Saruk insisted (wisely, as it turned out) that each merchant take a personal oath to keep his part of the bargain. On the other hand, there already was some sort of rudimentary communal organization in place. The rabbinic responsum from which we learn of this case notes that the Levantines already had some sort of *parnassim* or lay leaders; it was they who had approached Ben Saruk in the first place (*Responsa of R. Solomon de Medina*, IV, No. 99, c. 1571 in M. Goodblatt, 1952). Perhaps most important, the case makes it clear that the Levantine Jews were acting as a separate trade group in Venice, apparently without reference to the Armenians, Greeks and Turks who were in the city under exactly the same licence as they. While the Levantines may not yet have had a rabbi or some of the other services typical of a Jewish community, they had nevertheless begun the process of forming a political entity, one deriving from their special economic interests and, significantly, separate both from the non-Jewish world and from the Ashkenazi-Italiani moneylenders and second-hand dealers who had preceded them to Venice.

Of all the Levantine merchants in the last part of the sixteenth century, perhaps the best known was Daniel Rodriga. Feverishly enthusiastic, Rodriga was forever proposing new schemes, each grander than the last, and all aimed at making huge sums of money. At a distance of over four centuries it is hard now to decide how to treat Rodriga. Was he a bold visionary and grand entrepreneur or merely a self-indulgent chaser after dreams?

Whatever the final judgment of history, Rodriga could point to a number of successes. For example, he was behind the development of the port at Spalato (Split), then under Venetian control. Certainly the Venetian authorities felt Rodriga was a respectable merchant for by 1574 they had agreed to recognize him as the Levantines' elected consul. For the next fifteen years Rodriga petitioned repeatedly for expansions of his community's franchise in Venice, and finally, in 1589, his request was granted. From then on, there would be two legal Jewish communities living side-by-side in Venice: the 'German' and the Levantine, each with its own charter, and each with its own interests and concerns.

But the complexity of the Venetian Jewish community did not end here. Many, if not most, of the Levantine traders were Sephardic and Portuguese; that is, they traced their ancestry back to Jews who had once lived on the Iberian peninsula. While in some cases, the family had lived in the east for generations, in many other cases these were individuals who had decided to flee eastward and return to Judaism even though they and their ancestors had long lived as New Christians in Spain or Portugal.

These *conversos* presented difficult legal and policy problems to the Venetian authorities. Since they had been born as Christians and now practised Judaism these Iberians were, by traditional Church law, heretics, and as such were liable to the severest of penalties.

The Jews from the Levant were also Ottoman subjects and thus protected by the power and prestige of the Sublime Porte. To prosecute them, therefore, would mean not only to ruin an important source of commerce but also to risk war with the Turks. Venice opted for the wisdom of practicality and decided that she need not investigate how these Jews had lived previously. So long as the Levantines lived in the Ghetto and behaved as Jews, the city would simply ignore their past.

As the years went by, it became an open secret that more and more of Venice's 'Levantines' had never so much as been in the Ottoman Empire. Some had come directly from the Iberian peninsula; others had lived for a while as Christians in Florence, Rome or other western centres and now decided to declare their Jewishness to the world. Since both they and a very large proportion of the true Levantines spoke fluent Portuguese, the papal nuncio reported ruefully that it was often impossible to separate the two groups, even if the authorities had wished to do so. A few of the *conversos* took the precaution of more or less surreptitiously changing their western clothes for the flowing robes and turbans of the easterners just as their ship docked in Venice; others did not even bother with this minor pretence. All relied on the pragmatism of Venetian officials who continued to close their eyes, especially because among these newcomers were some of the wealthiest people of the day.

And yet one could not be too trusting. The Venetians might, after all, change their policy at any moment. Everyone remembered how Pope Paul IV had reversed decades of tolerant papal policy in Ancona, seized the former *conversos* living there and, in 1556 burned two dozen of them in a gruesome 'Act of Faith'. The intervention of the Ottoman Sultan had been of no help in that case, and the fact that the Jews had been able to organize a retaliatory boycott and cripple Ancona's port was of little comfort to the bereaved families.

It is no surprise, therefore, that Rodriga did his best to have the former *conversos* explicitly included in the *condotta*. The Venetians were wary of committing themselves formally to such a policy even though there were papal precedents which they could have cited for such a move. Rodriga therefore came up with an ingenious legal subterfuge to get around the problem. In a petition of 1583, this entrepreneur-turned-diplomat sought residence privileges not only for Levantines but also for 'Ponentines'.

This euphemism (which means west), innocuous enough in context, was directed straight at the former Christians from Portugal and Spain. Although that petition was refused, the same phrasing was repeated in the charter of 1589. The same charter which had finally given formal residence privileges to Levantine Jews in Venice, also gave such privileges to former New Christians who were willing to live in the Ghetto. In subsequent years a steady stream of Iberian New Christians would cautiously make their way to the Ghetto of Venice. There, famous physicians who had served royalty, learned jurists who had sat on some of the premier benches of Europe, scholars who had taught in leading universities, even men who had taken the vows of Christian priesthood, all of these would join together with hundreds, if not thousands of the less famous to rebuild the lost world of their Jewish ancestors.

Detail of a bench in the Scuola Grande Spagnola. According to ancient tradition, as old as the synagogues themselves, Venetian Jews can reserve their seats in the synagogue from one year to the next. Each place has a small plaque bearing the name of the person occupying the space. Often a family will occupy a whole bench and will have a box to hold their prayer shawls and prayer books.

Calle del Forno in the Ghetto Vecchio. The plaque marks the last house in the Ghetto. The buildings looking over the Fondamenta di Cannaregio, beside the Ghetto Vecchio, were inhabited by Christians. Their entrances were always placed outside the Ghetto boundary.

The year 1589 marks the completion of the Ghetto; not much would change over the next two hundred years. True, there would be one physical adjustment. In 1633 twenty more buildings – the so-called *ghetto nuovissimo* or newest ghetto – were incorporated into the Jews' living space. And legally, a few minor alterations would yet be made in the Jews' status. In 1634, for example, members of the 'German nation' were allowed for the first time to engage in the lucrative Levant trade. In 1738 the Venetian Senate abolished whatever legal distinctions remained between the two 'nations' by formally consolidating the two sets of *condotte*.

But in terms of its physical layout, its legal bases and, perhaps most important, the type of people who would inhabit it, the Ghetto of Venice was complete.

From the very beginning, the Jews of Venice complained that not enough space was being allocated to them. But the site of the foundry was so felicitous – if such a term can be used in urban planning – that the Jews' complaints were simply ignored. Located as it was on the northern edge of the city, the *ghetto nuovo* was not especially valuable real estate. The present landlords and tenants were easily placated, and the island contained no church or other sacred structure incompatible with the new purpose. Most especially to the point, the buildings there – a square constructed around a large central courtyard and in turn surrounded completely by water – already resembled a walled fortress. Only minor changes were needed to finish the enclosure, and controlling access would be relatively easy. The special three-man committee sent to look at the property found, as expected, that the existing flats in the block were 'most capacious' and could accommodate the roughly seven hundred Jews then in the city. The Jews did not agree. At least some of them actually left Venice rather than move into the new, tighter facility, while the community's unofficial spokesman, the wealthy Anselmo del Banco, offered 2000 ducats to be allowed to stay in his present housing – but all to no avail. Unfortunately the available data are often unreliable, and we do not really know just how many Jews lived in the cramped quarter at any given time. Conservative figures cite a population of 902 in the 1550s, 1,424 in the 1560s, and over 1,600 for most of the subsequent two centuries. Other records, however, suggest numbers twice and even three times as high. But even if we opt for the lower figures, it is clear that the Ghetto became ever more crowded with the passing years. According to one recent architectural survey, at times the Venetian Ghetto was so crowded that there was not enough floor space to allow all of its inhabitants the luxury of lying down at one time, and people must have had to sleep in shifts! (This was the finding of David Cassuto in a so-far unpublished paper which he delivered at the Cini Foundation's conference on the Jews and Venice.)

The Jews tried many different solutions to the problem of overcrowding. One approach was to divide up existing apartments to make room for more tenants. On lower floors which, by Italian urban custom, were reserved for commercial and storage facilities and for the homes of the very

poor, such divisions were accomplished horizontally: new flooring was inserted half-way between the existing floor and the ceiling. If the new apartments were dark, extra windows could be cut; these can sometimes still be seen today, climbing in an irregular series up the walls of the old buildings. But this could only partially alleviate the darkness. When Rabbi Leon Modena was forced by poverty and ill health to move into one of these 'dark and gloomy' apartments, he promptly dubbed it the 'Cave of Makhpelah' (after Genesis 23), and complained bitterly about the high rent he paid for living next to a store (Cohen, ed., *The Autobiography of a Seventeenth-Century Venetian Rabbi*, p. 156).

Another common method of dealing with overcrowding was to add storey after storey to the existing buildings until the Ghetto came to resemble nothing so much as an assemblage of towers. Even though this approach added significantly to the stock of housing, it did have one major drawback. Foundations originally laid to support two storeys above ground level were now being forced to hold as many as eight. Inevitably, the resulting structures sometimes collapsed, especially if too many people gathered for a party or celebration in a single home.

Wealthier individuals could try to acquire larger living facilities in other ways. Many, for example, added cantilevered balconies or roof-top 'belvederes' and patios to their apartments, a practice followed by Venetians in other parts of the city as well. The Jews were required to pay the city an annual tax for such 'extravagances' but were apparently willing to do so since the extensions provided both useful living space and, what was perhaps even more important, a view of the world outside the Ghetto. And of course, we must not forget that the Venetian authorities proved willing to add to the stock of Jewish housing when the new facilities might help attract trade to the city. Both the *ghetto vecchio* and the *ghetto nuovissimo* were incorporated into the Jewish quarter at the request of merchants. Indeed, archival records show that in the 1630s, when the last of these expansions took place, there actually were empty apartments in the Ghetto. The community was able to obtain the new flats only by posting a 3000-ducat bond to be forfeited should twenty families of wealthy immigrants not move to the city during the first year.

Within the perimeter of these three linked quarters thousands of Jews made their home; Italiani and French, Yiddish-speaking Ashkenazim and Spanish- or Portuguese-speaking Sephardim, Levantines and Ponentines, all rubbed shoulders with each other and with the not infrequent visitors from every corner of the Jewish world. The cacophony of daily life under such conditions, the intense heterogeneity of existence must have seemed overwhelming at times. And, paradoxically, far from encouraging uniformity, the narrow parameters of life in the Ghetto seem to have led to a constant reiteration of ethnic divergence. If only to survive, each group felt compelled to emphasize its own particularism, to form a smaller society within the whole, with its own synagogue and ritual, fraternal organization and charities. It is to an examination of the diversity of life in the Ghetto which we must now turn our attention.

Because of the severe shortage of space in the Ghetto, houses were gradually built up to heights unrivalled anywhere else in Venice.

Wealth divided the Ghetto horizontally and determined the floor on which one lived and the square metres over which one's life could extend. Ethnicity divided the Ghetto vertically and was in many ways a more important determinant of how one passed the day. To the Venetian authorities the Jews of the Ghetto were separated into two 'nations' – the 'German' and the Levantine-Ponentine. Inside the Ghetto, the situation was more complex. For political purposes, the Levantines and Ponentines constituted separate communities which might, or might not, be joined in accordance with the needs of the moment. For religious purposes, even the German nation was split. Italian Jews had their own synagogue and authorities, their own confraternities and ritual customs, and their own very clear sense of a separate identity. And of course there were also varying numbers of French, *Romaniyot* or Greek, and North African Jews who were forced to find a place for themselves within the cultural mosaic. Behind high walls, the Jews had to develop new mechanisms for dealing with ethnic diversity and religious difference, with political rivalry and economic competition, and, for that matter, with the sort of 'tribal' prejudice from which they were no more immune than other societies.

Perhaps most sensitive to slight were the Italiani Jews who must have seen themselves as the community's proper leaders but who had been displaced by the other larger, and often wealthier, communities. One hears the underlying resentment in a responsum by Rabbi Judah Arye Modena in which he defends the legitimacy of the Italiani custom of not covering the head except during prayers.

Most of this community, and most Italiani Jews, do not customarily [cover their heads], and I felt it was important to tell them that this was permissible. I would do the same thing concerning several other matters about which Italiani Jews are attacked and concerning which the great scholars among us should either rule that they are permitted or [at least] should explain [the Italiani custom] and not concede to the Levantines and Ashkenazim that we are heretics and they are pious Jews. The Lord spoke to us as well, and we and our children accept and love His written and oral law for all time. (*Responsa of R. Juda Arye Modena*, ed. S. Simonsohn, responsum 21, p. 36 f.)

The synagogue itself became a primary focus of ethnic identity and rivalry. The five beautiful renaissance-baroque synagogues which, for all the neglect they have endured, are still the showpieces of the Venetian Ghetto each grew out of a community's intense need to express its identity through architecture and architectural adornment. First came the aptly named Scuola Grande Tedesca of the Ashkenazim (1528) whose large hall with its five arched windows would accommodate the meetings of the Great Assembly throughout the ghetto period. There were also two smaller synagogues in the *ghetto nuovo*, the Ashkenazi Scuola Canton (1531) whose precise origins are now lost, and the Scuola Italiana (1571) in which the growing Italiani Jewish community was able to follow its own traditions. And then came the two large synagogues in the *ghetto vecchio*

The Scuola Canton, showing the cupola. The origins of the name are still debated.

– that of the Levantines and that of the Ponentines. Especially the latter structure, the Scuola Grande Spagnola, built in 1584 and then completely refurbished in 1635, is a striking statement of the wealth and self-confidence of Venetian Sephardim for all that they lived in a ghetto.

The Ponentines were eager to have their synagogue become the central building of the Ghetto and insisted on pride of place for it. In 1651, therefore, they argued that the public ceremonies celebrating the completion of a Talmudic tractate by the Ghetto's study group be held completely in their synagogue. The Ashkenazi Jews complained, pointing out that by tradition the classes had always been split: in summer they had been held in the Scuola Grande Tedesca, while in winter they had moved into the Sephardic synagogue. Correspondingly, they felt, the ceremonies should now be divided. So aggrieved were the Ashkenazim that they commissioned Isaac min ha-

Levi'im (grandson of R. Judah Arye Modena) to write a song (or perhaps a short oratorio) defending their position. The Sephardim of course responded in kind. According to *their* composer, the long-standing custom of dividing the classes between the communities had been nothing more than an act of graciousness on the part of the Sephardim. (The Sephardim also immediately fired the unfortunate Isaac min ha-Levi'im who had held a minor clerical post in one of their societies.) A wiser rabbi, Azariah Picho, had been careful not to challenge the power of the Sephardim. In his inaugural sermon as rabbi of the Ponentine 'Holy Community Talmud Torà' a few years earlier, Picho had almost obsequiously acknowledged their authority. In lifting him up from his former 'lowly position' as rabbi of Pisa, the Venetians could be compared to God himself, 'for this is also His way to lift up the lowly.' (Azariah Picho (Figo), *Sefer Bina le-Itim* Venice: 1648/9 or 1652/3), first sermon.)

Of course, the major arena in which ethnic identity had to be addressed was in the composition of the Ghetto's governing bodies, bodies which had now to deal with issues of municipal government in addition to more traditional concerns. The main deliberative body, the 'Great Assembly' (*Va'ad Gadol*), was open to all Jewish adult males who paid annual taxes of at least 12 ducats, but the three committees which handled day-to-day administration were carefully organized to reflect the interests and power of the different groups within the community. This was equally true for the executive 'Small Assembly' (*va'ad katan*), for 'The Twenty', charged with overseeing the loanbanks which the Jews ran for the poor of Venice, and for the 'Assessors' (*tan-sadori* or *ma'arikhim*) who set the level of each individual's tax payment to the community. A recent survey of political development in the early seventeenth century shows that Venetian Jewry was almost obsessively concerned with the ethnic representativeness of these committees, and that the communal constitution was re-written time after time in order to achieve an acceptable balance. Although the Ghetto's first inhabitants, the Ashkenazi-Italiani group, remained the single largest and most powerful political bloc, they were forced to cede a significant degree of authority to an alliance of Ponentines and Levantines. Within the latter bloc, moreover, the Ponentines grew in stature, outstripping the Levantines and eventually becoming almost as powerful as the Ashkenazi-Italiani Jews. In passing we might note that a similar ethnic rivalry in the Roman ghetto ended with the clear-cut dominance of the Italiani-Ashkenazic bloc. In Livorno, on the other hand, the Sephardim were able to keep the Ashkenazi and Italiani Jews almost completely disenfranchised.

At one and the same time cut off from Venice and yet integrated into that city's life, the Ghetto formed a shadow world in which identity was not always clear and lines of demarcation not always sharp. Superficial devices like the coloured hats – yellow for Ashkenazim and red for Sephardim – with which city officials

Interior of the Scuola Grande Spagnola, the synagogue in longest continuous use in the Ghetto.

Calle del Forno in the Ghetto Vecchio. During Passover, the Jewish Easter, a special oven is used for baking bread and sweets, under the supervision of the rabbi. The sweetmeats are not only consumed in Venice, but are exported to cities all over Italy.

tried to mark the Jews could not cope with the complex categories of individuality into which people fell. There were, first of all, the converts — often marginal figures but sometimes, as in the case of the brothers de Freschi Olivi, medical doctors and substantial members of both worlds. On the one hand, the Jews tended to dismiss the sincerity of such converts. 'Someone who was not a good Jew cannot be a good Christian,' sniffed a certain Ashkenazi music teacher named Salamone when asked about the converts by the city's Inquisition. On the other hand, the Jews hated such converts and feared the ruin they might cause in their often compulsive efforts to legitimize their own act of abandonment. Giovanni Battista de Freschi Olivi, for example, had been active in denouncing the Talmud and having it burned in the 1550s, and he knew that 'all of the Jews in the world are my enemies.' But if conversion had removed these Jews from their native community, it could not fully integrate them into their new surroundings. The Christian community would not forget their Jewish origins and suspected them always of plotting against Christian values. When the brothers'

mother, Elena, became senile and began muttering blasphemies to herself and making obscene gestures towards the priest at every mention of the Virgin Mary, she was not tolerated with a smile as were many others who had had the good fortune of being born into the Church. In the case of this old woman, the Church ordered her to be jailed for two years and then spend the rest of her life locked alone in a room in her son's home.

More complex yet was the situation of the Iberian New Christians. 'People on the frontier between Christianity and Judaism' is what one recent study has aptly called them, people who often would not, perhaps could not, choose between the two faiths (Brian Pullan, *The Jews of Europe and the Inquisition of Venice 1550–1670*). Not a few of these immigrants — and sometimes the very wealthiest and best known among them — opted to live as Christians in Venice only to be caught 'judaizing' elsewhere or, worse yet, in the local ghetto. In other cases, the New Christians would suddenly disappear, and then months later rumours would come back to the city that they had been sighted living as Jews in Istanbul or Saloniki, beyond the reach of the law. Such renegades were a serious threat to the religiously structured society of Venice, and those in authority continued to expel them as a group and prosecute them individually throughout the sixteenth and seventeenth centuries.

But many other *conversos* opted, as we have seen, to join the Jewish community and live in the Ghetto. This group also challenged Christian society, though there was frustratingly little that could be done about them. An inquisitorial record of 1654 records two friars walking near the Ghetto who were suddenly approached, in Spanish, by a Jewish street vendor. When they asked about the Jew's language skills and background, he cheerfully told them with a wink and a gesture to his red cap, that he was a native of Madrid and had moved to Venice in order to wear a Cardinal's hat! The humour was undoubtedly lost on the outraged clerics.

What is often forgotten is that such *conversos* also presented a serious challenge to the Jewish society in the ghetto. For the Jews, and especially for those who had once lived as Christians before coming to live in the ghetto, there was a constant need to re-confirm the superiority of Judaism

and hence to re-validate their own decision. Their choice was legitimized if they could convince others to follow in their path; their choice was left open to doubt if others refused. The soul of each New Christian became, in effect, a battle ground in the ongoing war for metaphysical legitimacy, and huge resources were thrown into the battle for souls. Money was raised to ease the transition, the basic texts of Judaism were translated into Spanish, and those who had made the transition wrote and preached continuously about the spiritual satisfaction they had found. Rabbi Samuel Aboab, himself from a *converso* family, urged the formation of special societies to sponsor the Jewish education of 'those who come from servitude to spiri-

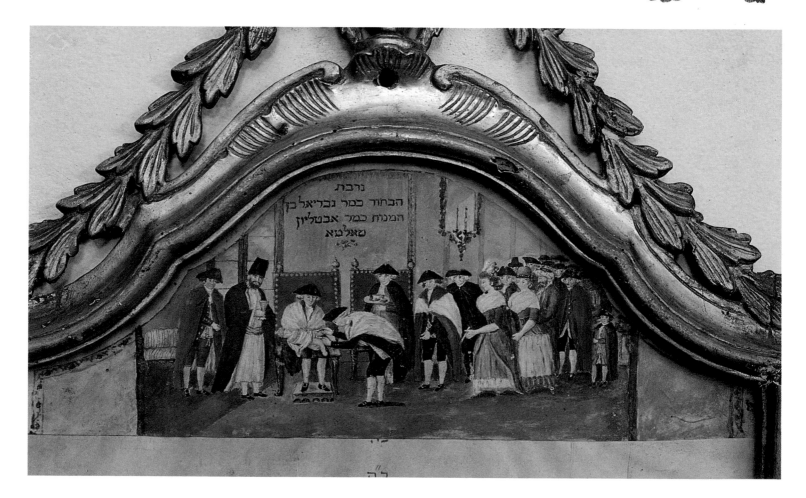

A scene from Jewish life in Venice. A circumcision in the late eighteenth century, with messages of good luck for the baby. An old man, presumably the grandfather, holding an eight day old baby in his arms, whilst a specialized surgeon performs the circumcision, the *Mila*. Interestingly, the only person wearing a special headdress is the Rabbi (second from the left), all the other men wearing the traditional Venetian tricorn. The women are wearing fashionable clothes. The empty seat is awaiting the arrival of the prophet Elijah; custom has it that he symbolically presides over the ceremony. (Museum of Jewish Art).

tual liberation, and from pitch and utter darkness to the pure light of the Torah ...' Even if the New Christian remained within the Jewish community, the struggle was not over. Because the newcomer had not grown up amid an organic, functioning Judaism, he or she might often question accepted interpretations of sacred scripture, mock the irrationality of traditional customs and read his own interpretations into Jewish rites and commandments. Such interpretations were often heavily influenced by Christian values and concepts. Circumcision, for example, went from a ceremony marking the covenant between God and the Jewish people to a rite of induction which, like Christian baptism, wiped away sin. This was not an empty theological debate. If circumcision washed away sin, then it could be delayed until the end of one's life. Since atonement was available, the New Christian could continue to slide between the two worlds and to resume a Christian identity should that prove convenient. The Jewish community was no more able to tolerate such a double identity than was the Christian. And yet, more than a few of the newcomers remained, as one contemporary put it, 'like a ship with two rudders' forever suspended between Christianity and Judaism.

When French forces invaded Italy at the end of the eighteenth century, the Ghetto's Jews contributed generously to the defence of their beloved Venice. But the limited toleration of a ghetto had no place in the new political order announced by those who had stormed the Bastille. In the world of liberty, equality and fraternity, no one could be enclosed behind walls on account of religion —

no matter how comfortable the cell. In July, 1797, therefore, the French forces pulled down the gates and erected a liberty tree in the central courtyard of what had been the most famous ghetto in Europe.

Today the streets of the Venetian ghetto are quiet. The afternoon sun discovers a few tourists, a pensioner or two chatting on a public bench, a member of the dwindling local Jewish community making his or her way to the synagogue or communal offices. It is hard to remember that the scene *piazza* once echoed with thousands of voices. Under the porticos hawkers cried in hoarse dialects and women chatted as they washed and darned bits of used clothing for resale in the shops; merchants haggled over the prices of leather and silk from east and west, while Christian priests and Jewish rabbis debated the relative merits of their two faiths with similar avidity and zeal.

The Jews came to Venice in waves, drawn to land as were the waves of the Adriatic, periodically rising, engulfing the city's 'streets' and then mixing with the older waters. From the small towns of the Veneto and from the courts of Europe, from the open fields of the North and the bazaars of the Orient – from all these places and a hundred more, the Jews came to build a true metropolis of diversity in the *hatzer* or courtyard of the Venetian Ghetto. And in the end they succeeded. Menasseh ben Israel could think of no better model when he urged Cromwell to admit the Jews to England in 1654. For him and the rest of Europe, the city of Venice was the Jews' 'principal residence' in Italy. And for all that they lived in a ghetto, added the rabbi, 'they are used there with much courtesy and clemency.'

A Tour of
the Ghetto

Roberta Curiel

Translated by Caroline Beamish

THE GHETTO NUOVO

If you walk away from the busy Rio Terà San Leonardo in a north-westerly direction, first along the Rio Terà Farsetti, then across the *caleselle* (one of the lanes of Venice, also known as *calle* or *callette*), you will arrive at one of the three entrances to the Ghetto Nuovo. A compact group of houses, some of them eight storeys high, rises up suddenly before you. Rows and rows of windows lead your gaze upwards to the sky.

A small wooden bridge, rather like the drawbridge of a medieval castle, and a narrow '*sotopòrtego*' (a passageway through a building) connect the restricted, secluded world of the Ghetto to the outside world. Holes in the Istrian stone can easily be seen on either side of the entrance to the *sotopòrtego*, in which were fixed the hinges of one of the wooden gates which from 1516 to 1797 isolated the Jewish quarter from the rest of the city at night.

This was the site chosen by the Venetian Senate, after lengthy deliberation: a small island in the San Girolamo district, around which a wall was built. On 29 March 1516 all Jews were ordered to come and live within the wall; they were to return to the Ghetto at night and were to be responsible for paying the guards who kept a twenty-four-hour watch on the gates and patrolled the canals in small boats.

The entrance to the Ghetto Nuovo from the *caleselle*. Originally two wooden gates were fixed to the sides of the doorway.

Page 28 A view from the centre of the Campo del Ghetto Nuovo, showing its most important side. On the right is the modest outline of the Scuola Grande Tedesca.

The wooden bridge over the Rio del Ghetto Nuovo leads into the enclosed world of the Ghetto.

Just before the *sotopòrtego*, on the right, the frame of a small walled-up window beside the bridge recalls the time when Christian watchmen, possibly from this vantage point, kept a constant watch on those entering and leaving the Ghetto.

Almost from the outset, Jewish doctors were the only people allowed to leave the Ghetto during the night, either to visit their Christian patients, often people of importance, or to consult with their colleagues. They were also permitted to wear black caps rather than the yellow caps (later red) worn by other members of the Jewish community to facilitate identification.

Between 1517 and 1721 at least two hundred and fifty Jewish medical students graduated at the University of Padua, the central university of the Veneto. Many other Jewish doctors from Spain and

Resembling the drawbridge of a medieval castle, this is the most impressive of the three entrances to the Ghetto.

Portugal came to practise their profession in the secure environment of the Serenissima. In the second half of the sixteenth century the distinguished Jewish doctor David de' Pomis became the official medical adviser to the City of Venice and a favourite of the powerful Cardinal Grimani.

From the *sotopòrtego* we emerge into the broad, bright Campo del Ghetto Nuovo, the 'square of the new foundry'. In earlier days it was more generally known by its inhabitants as the 'chazèr', or garden. Its almost circular shape vaguely recalls the Piazza del Mercato in Lucca. The squares of Venice are called *campi*, the Piazza San Marco being considered the only square worthy of the name *piazza*. Originally the *campi* were unpaved; the paths that crossed them were of beaten earth, the rest of the square being either grassed, or under cultivation. This *campo* is one of the largest and quietest in the Cannaregio with shade provided by some large trees, a fountain, some marble benches and a few small souvenir shops.

The gates to the Ghetto remained open by day, guarded by watchmen. When the gates were closed at night the isolation of the Ghetto was almost complete.

The dark narrow passageway of the Sotopòrtego del Ghetto Nuovo emphasizes the spaciousness and brightness of the large Campo. It is quiet and peaceful today, but in the past it was alive with bustling throngs of people.

The 'skyscrapers' are a well-known feature of the Campo del Ghetto Nuovo. Underneath is the Sotopòrtego del Banco Rosso.

A nocturnal view of the Ghetto Nuovo, as seen in the famous love scene in *Senso*, Luchino Visconti's cinematic masterpiece.

It is immediately clear that something to be found in the great majority of Venetian squares is here conspicuous by its absence. The visitor's eye searches in vain for the façade of a church, be it grand or humble. Also absent are those elegant, sober palaces that enhance almost all the other squares in Venice, as for example at San Paolo or at Santo Stefano.

The buildings here, particularly the façade above the *sotopòrtego*, make a big block, plain without being dull. The walls are enlivened by innumerable windows of all shapes and sizes, little terraces and gables, with a few small domes, slightly oriental in character, long arcades and some lower buildings, only one or two storeys high, which lean higgledy-piggledy against their much taller neighbours.

This extraordinary frontage was used by Luchino Visconti as the setting for a night scene in his film *Senso* (one of the most intense scenes in the film), made in 1954 from the story of the same name by Camillo Boito; it makes an unforgettable impression.

If you look carefully at this façade it becomes obvious that some of the apartments, still inhabited today, must have extremely low ceilings, in most of the lower floors less than six feet (two metres) high. Look through the open doors and you can see steep, narrow staircases – deathtraps in the event of a fire, and the Ghetto, as we now know, was frequently subject to fires. One does not have to look far for the reason for such curious town planning. Jacopo de' Barbari's celebrated perspective map of Venice, engraved in 1500, shows that the small island of Ghetto Nuovo, where there was an arms foundry until about 1390, was already completely built up by the end of the fifteenth century, with two-storey buildings all around its perimeter. Following the traditional design of a Venetian house, which remained unchanged for centuries, the ground floor consisted of a storeroom for provisions, with servants' quarters and kitchens on the first floor, then living quarters for the family on the *piano nobile* above.

From 29 March 1516 onwards, the small island of Ghetto Nuovo, covering an area of about 17 acres (7,000 square metres), was to become the obligatory home of the Jewish community. At first there were about seven hundred inhabitants, mainly German Jews who had been living in the Veneto for years, and Italian Jews from central southern Italy. But these numbers were to increase very rapidly: at one period, between the last decades of the sixteenth century and the first of the seventeenth, there were up to two thousand people living there.

Three thousand of the seven thousand square metres which make up the island are contained in the Campo, so it is not difficult to imagine that lack of space was a grave problem. It should also be remembered that the ground-floor apartments were usually either shops, stores or pawnbrokers. Space was also needed for schools and meeting places, including places of worship. The vertical use of space, by the construction of tall houses, must have taken place during the first hundred or hundred and twenty years after the foundation of the Ghetto. In some cases the existing ground floor was divided into half horizontally, making the resulting rooms usable only as service areas or storerooms as the ceilings were sometimes lower than 5 feet $10\frac{1}{2}$ inches (180 cm) high.

The soil of Venice is not firm enough to bear the weight of very tall buildings. Although the walls have been reinforced at ground level, and the internal construction of the dwellings is of wood where possible (wood being a light building material), cracks in the fabric can be seen everywhere. A contemporary chronicle describes a wedding feast during which the floor gave way under the weight of the guests.

Old house in the Ghetto Vecchio. Narrow, irregular windows give animation to the plain façades, and provide sudden, unexpected light and shade effects.

Accommodation was perhaps the most difficult problem that a Jewish family had to face, and we know that when housing became vacant an announcement would be made in the synagogue. Jews were prohibited by law from owning property but a special regulation, known as the *jus gazaka* (the name is a mixture of Latin and Hebrew, and can be roughly translated as 'right of possession'), established that rents could not be increased under any pretext, nor could a tenant be evicted. If a person was in short-term financial difficulties, the community would come to his assistance. This inalienable right of residence was hereditary, and it played a vital role in maintaining the conditions of life in the Ghetto at a reasonable level.

Many foreign visitors to Venice, a tourist city throughout its existence, penetrated the walls of the Ghetto, attracted by the exotic nature of the area and the beauty of the synagogues, and also curious to see the tall buildings in this 'citadel within a city' with their own eyes. The island was surrounded on all sides by gardens and vegetable plots, the only buildings of any size in the neighbourhood being the Convents of San Girolamo and Santa Maria dei Servi, so the impression that the tower-houses of the Jewish quarter must have made on travellers in the past can easily be imagined.

More recently, in the early years of this century, the writer and poet Rainer Maria Rilke, after a visit to Venice, wrote a story about an old Jew in the Ghetto who dreamed of living on the top floor of the tallest building; from his window he imagined that he would be able, when the quarter was liberated, to discern the open sea in the distance ('A Scene from the Ghetto in Venice' from *Stories of God*).

It is on the top floor, up in the sky, that the three oldest synagogues in Venice are to be found, huddled side by side and connected by a system of internal passageways which still exists today. The *halacha*, the law governing Jewish ritual, stipulates that the synagogue must be built 'in the highest part of the city'; this rule may be intended to isolate the synagogue from everyday life, thereby giving it greater dignity and distance. It is also of fundamental ritual importance that those in the *beth-ha-knesset*, the meeting and prayer room, should be able to see the sky and the stars; therefore nothing should be built above the prayer room to come between those praying and the sky. The Jewish community of the Ghetto, keen to abide by the commandments of their faith, solved the problem in the only way possible. They raised their synagogues above the existing buildings, adapting their size and shape to the narrow space available in the Ghetto Nuovo between the Campo (the social and economic centre of the quarter) and the canal that surrounds the small island.

Aside from purely religious reasons, it is plain that the notion of building the synagogues at the top of existing dwellings must have seemed a reasonable kind of precaution for a foreign community, not fully integrated into the city, to take, particularly in times that were amongst the most troubled in Venetian history. To have built highly visible buildings, exposed to the sometimes inimical gaze of the neighbouring Christian population, might have provoked trouble, even though the government kept a watchful eye on the community. Venice at the time was often prey to violently antisemitic preachers, who might have incited the populace against the Jews in their midst.

To make unwelcome visits even less likely, the staircases leading to the synagogues, as well as to the private dwellings, were extremely long, steep and dark, making the prayer rooms even more like eagles' nests. The two synagogues in the Ghetto Vecchio, the Scuola Spagnola and the Scuola Levantina, differ from the Scuole of the Ghetto Nuovo because they were rebuilt around the middle of the seventeenth century, at a moment of relative calm for the Jewish community in Venice, reflected in the difference in their external appearance. Their greater external elegance can be attributed to the fact that by the time they were constructed the presence of the Jews in Venice was an accepted fact, hallowed by tradition, and therefore the community no longer felt itself threatened.

A Jew from G. Grevembroch, *The Customs of the Venetians*, Museo Civico Correr, Venice.

Previous page Campo del Ghetto Nuovo. The tall, close-knit group of dwellings is unique in the Venetian skyline.

Sotopòrtego del Banco Rosso. Besides the pawnbrokers' shops, the Campo contained dozens of shops selling old clothes, or 'strazzaria', of which there were sixty or so in the eighteenth century.

THE SCUOLA GRANDE TEDESCA

The walls in marbling and wood, and the Venetian tiled floor, date from the sixteenth and seventeenth centuries. The *bimah* and the women's gallery bear the hallmarks of the eighteenth century.

The façade of the Scuola Grande Tedesca, easily identifiable by the row of five windows. On the right the door of the Museum of Jewish Art can be seen.

Unless you knew of their existence it would be difficult to guess that there are three synagogues in the Campo del Ghetto Nuovo, the Scuola Grande Tedesca, the Scuola Canton and the Scuola Italiana, as their exteriors are camouflaged amongst the busy façades of the houses in the Campo. The easiest one to spot from outside is perhaps the Scuola Grande Tedesca, on the left of the *sotopòrtego* with its five arched windows (two of them now bricked up) framed in Istrian stone, and a prominent inscription in Hebrew immediately below the cornice.

The five-window motif, repeated on the main façade of the Scuola Canton, along the canal, and on the nearby Scuola Italiana, has a very precise religious significance: the Torah, the book of divine law, is divided into five books. A parchment manuscript of the Torah, copied in the ancient way using special ink, is kept inside the synagogue in an Ark always facing towards Jerusalem. The inscription below the cornice records that the building was first put up in 1528–29 (5289 of the Jewish era) and was rebuilt in 1732–33. Lower down is another inscription, still in Hebrew, which reads: 'The Scuola Grande of the sacred community of Germans, whom God protect. Amen'.

Half-way through the fourteenth century many Ashkenazi Jews from the northern part of Europe, especially from France and Germany, began moving south. The population of Europe was in turmoil after the Black Death in 1348, for which Jews were often made the scapegoat and were accused of poisoning the water in the wells. Groups of Ashkenazi Jews began to gather in the Veneto and throughout the north of Italy. These groups were frequently given permission to set up as moneylenders, an occupation then forbidden to Christians by the Church.

Below the five windows of the Scuola Tedesca there are some modest dwellings which are inhabited to this day; through their small windows a glimpse can be caught of the very low-ceilinged rooms.

Access to the German Synagogue today is by the same staircase that leads to the Museum of Jewish Art, a valuable collection of sacred objects (see p. 157). The stairs were rebuilt in 1848, as recorded by the inscription on the first landing, to replace the original very steep and narrow staircase. The same thing occurred shortly afterwards at the nearby Scuola Canton.

The entrance to the synagogue from one corner allows the visitor to appreciate at once the light, almost frivolous elegance of the women's gallery and the sumptuous gilding (recently restored); by comparison the woodwork covering the lower part of the walls is severe. Closer study of the upper gallery reveals the fact that the oval effect is achieved by *trompe l'oeil* techniques: it is not oval, as it appears, but trapezoid in shape, the side facing the canal being considerably longer than the side

on the Campo (44 x 28 x 42 x 22 feet/13.4 x 8.7 x 12.9 x 6.7 metres). This asymmetry is evidently due to practical problems, but it has been exploited by the anonymous architect in such a way as to produce unusual and interesting perspectives; many bridges in Venice have been built in a similar fashion, crossing the canals at an oblique angle for reasons of space. If you look at this room from the four corners in turn it looks interestingly different from each one.

Other incongruities strike the visitor, besides the irregularity of the four walls and the curious perspectives that result from it. What is a little covered skylight doing in the centre of the ceiling? And why is the text of the Ten Commandments, inscribed on a band of gold and red around the walls, interrupted in one place? Why is there an empty space in the middle of the Venetian paving on the floor? These mysteries can be solved with a little imagination if we interpret the scant information available today on the history of the restoration and alteration of the synagogue over the years.

This synagogue was certainly built onto an existing building, possibly in the fifteenth century. Although it is the oldest synagogue in the Ghetto, little trace remains of the original fifteenth-century

The gilded wood of the eighteenth-century women's gallery in the Scuola Grande Tedesca. Oval in shape, its *trompe l'oeil* effect helps minimize the asymmetrical shape of the room. In the centre of the ceiling is a lantern, covered over in the nineteenth century.

An exterior view of the Scuola Grande Tedesca on the Rio del Ghetto Nuovo. Here again the shape of the Ark of the Covenant inside projects over the canal.

An interior view of the Scuola Grande Tedesca taken from the Ark. Against the back wall is the *bimah*, originally in the centre of the chamber but now placed against the wall opposite the Ark.

decoration. Expert opinion has it that the floor, typical Venetian paving in marble mosaic, had not been restored until a few years ago. The walnut benches, which are beautifully decorated with carved flowers and animals (the lion's paws are worthy of note) are possibly from the late sixteenth century. The walls, marbled above and covered in cherry wood below, are similar to walls constructed in the sixteenth and seventeenth centuries in the halls of certain religious communities – the famous Scuole – as well as in sacristies and study rooms all over Venice. There, as in the Scuola Tedesca, a bench is fixed to the wall all round the room, giving unity and dignity to the whole. The same or similar treatment can be found in the upper room of the Scuola de Carmini, and in S. Giovanni Evangelista, as well as in the Scuola Dalmata of S. Giorgio and S. Trifone.

There is however a difference between the Scuola Tedesca and the Christian Scuole or sacristies: here the austere panels in dark wood are not surmounted by paintings on religious themes, such as for instance the panels by Carpaccio in the Scuola Dalmata. The Jewish religion forbids the portrayal of the human body inside the synagogue, which makes the display of paintings on edifying and didactic themes difficult, if not impossible. Inscriptions on the walls are used instead. Venetian sumptuary laws, regularly imposed to control the use of luxurious materials such as marble, explain the *trompe l'oeil* marbling of the upper panels. There is a more liberal and ostentatious use of marble in the two later synagogues in the Ghetto Vecchio. In theory the Venetian law governing the lives of its Jewish inhabitants maintained that each city could have only one synagogue, without any external decoration, furnished internally with 'poor' materials such as wood, or fake marble. Evidently the law was never particularly rigorously applied.

Scuola Grande Tedesca: a detail of the exterior facing onto the Rio del Ghetto Nuovo.

It is not easy to give an exact date to the wall decorations: the cherry-wood panelling, with its simple, traditional patterns based on rectangles and hexagons, probably dates from the first period before the rebuilding in the mid-seventeenth century. Certainly the red border bearing the text of the Ten Commandments from the book of Exodus is very old; this, with the chairbacks and the marbled panels, gives a visual unity to the whole space below the oval women's gallery. The continuous text is unique in the Venetian synagogues as an architectural device (it joins the four walls together and separates the women's gallery from the rest of the building); the text does not appear in any of the other four Scuole, and is rare in Italy and indeed in the whole of Europe.

The *aaron hakodesh* certainly belongs to the later building phase: this is a structure in three parts, the middle part housing the Ark which contains the manuscript of the Pentateuch (the Torah in Hebrew), and two decorated stalls on either side.

One of the four steps in red marble bears an inscription recording that the Ark was a gift from 'the elder of the Zemel brothers, the rabbi Menachem Cividale, son of rabbi Joseph. 5432 (1672)'. The earlier *aaron* was probably smaller because the present one covers part of one of the decorative rosettes on the floor. The central part of the present *aaron* juts out of the east wall, overhanging the canal that borders the Ghetto Nuovo. The broken tympanum, in the Palladian style, is decorated with carved urns and cornucopias, supported by two Corinthian columns. The double door (symbolizing the Tablets of the Law) bears an elegantly stylized tree of life carved on the outside. Inside, the Ten Commandments, inlaid in mother-of-pearl, are topped by a coronet, symbolizing the paramountcy of the Law of God. The '*ner tamid*', or eternal flame, burns in front of the doors of the Ark as a perpetual reminder of holiness.

On either side of the *aaron* are two seats for the *parnassim*, the wise elders who administer the synagogue; the seats are richly carved with floral designs and have backs upholstered in red. On the backs are didactic inscriptions: on the right: 'Where the ancients sit there shall He be praised', and on the left: 'Who sits in unity becomes also wise'.

The Ark of the Covenant is entirely covered by a sheet of gold: the gilding was probably inspired by the cover for the sacred objects in the temple in Jerusalem, also gold. The combination of the gold and the warm tones of the woodwork gives a rich and festive atmosphere.

The *bimah* here is also gilded. It is a raised platform or pulpit for the officiating rabbi. Another term for the *bimah* is the '*almemar*', from the Arabic *al mimbar*, or 'place from which prayers and hymns are said'. In this synagogue it is against the wall opposite the Ark, facing the

The Ark of the Covenant is a three-part structure. The central part is the Ark containing the scrolls of the Torah. The seats on either side were reserved for the *parnassim*, or elders, of the synagogue.

Detail of the pediment over the Ark. The broken tympanum is decorated with cornucopias and urns.

Inside the doors of the Ark, on either side, the opening words of the Ten Commandments are inlaid in mother of pearl. The crown symbolizes the supremacy of the Divine Law.

The doors of the Ark of the Covenant in the Scuola Grande Tedesca are decorated with stylized versions of the Tree of Life.

Campo del Ghetto. Stylistically the *bimah* is related to both the Ark and to the entrance portal, reiterating the vase design found above the doors. Elements from the women's gallery are also to be found here: the little stylized capitals from the parapet, and the pattern of circles and rectangles. The *bimah*, like the Ark, has columns with Corinthian capitals, but the bases of the columns on the *bimah* are bulbous, and decorated with leaf designs; they are probably a little later. From the *bimah* the leader of prayer reads the sacred texts, says the prayers and blesses the congregation. In the German tradition, and generally in Central Europe, it was a light structure placed centrally with enough space around it to allow movement all round. This type of structure can be found throughout northern Italy in synagogues belonging to German communities, for example in Cherasco, Carmagnola, Casal Monferrato.

The German Jews of Venice clearly followed this tradition at the outset. The *bimah* in the Scuola Tedesca was originally placed in the middle of the room, away from the wall; it was only later moved to stand against the back wall. It began life as an octagon, but then one of its sides was sawn off and the resulting trapezoid structure was leant against the wall: aesthetically a somewhat dubious solution to the problem. This is thought to explain the gap in the rosette patterns on the floor, and also the octagonal opening in the centre of the ceiling, both echoing the octagonal shape of the original *bimah*. Through the ceiling lantern, which at first was unroofed, the person officiating at the service would be able to see the sky and the stars. The effect created by light pouring down on the gilding and on all the rich baroque decorations can be imagined and with it the mystical effect on the souls of those gathered together in prayer.

Later, probably around 1860 when further restoration was undertaken, an important change was made: the sunlight and the rain began to annoy those leading the prayers and thus, after centuries, this synagogue followed the example of the other four synagogues in the Ghetto (and most other synagogues in Venice) and scrapped the central *bimah*. The *bimah* was placed directly in front of the Ark and the seats were rearranged along the walls in such a way as to leave a wide passageway down the centre. Later, probably in an attempt to prevent the entry of rainwater, a roof with wide eaves was erected over the lantern. The little cupola with its graceful columns can still be seen from inside, but nowadays it is useless because it lets no light in, unlike the cupolas on the neighbouring Scuola Canton and the Scuola Italiana, which can be seen from the outside as well. The removal of the *bimah* to the side wall led to the bricking up of two of the five windows that look out over the Campo; their outlines are still clearly visible from outside.

It is possible that when the *bimah* was in the centre of the room it may have been surmounted by a baldaquin, or by posts rising above it at an angle to meet overhead in a pyramid shape. Canopies of this kind can be found at Cherasco, at Carmagnola and, further away, in Poland. Such a canopy may have been discarded in order to fit the *bimah* under the oval women's gallery. This gallery gives the impression of weighing too heavily upon the slender, somewhat frail structure of the *bimah*. The stylized, gilded columns of the *bimah* are repeated on the irregular oval of the women's gallery; the gallery follows the shape of the room and as a result is wider and flatter on the east side, narrower on the Campo side. Seen from the door, however, it looks pleasant enough and is the unifying element of a very disparate whole. Various motifs recur here, such as the pattern of circles and rectangles from the parapet which we first noticed on the base of the *bimah*. The little columns on the parapet of the women's gallery recall those on the *bimah* and those on the lantern as well; in the latter case the columns are purely for ornament as nobody could follow the action from the lantern or its parapet. The

The interior of the Scuola Grande Tedesca, seen from the *bimah*: in the background, the eighteenth-century Ark. The synagogue is nowadays only used for special occasions such as weddings.

presence of so many slender columns gives a vitality, almost frivolity, to the whole of the upper part, which contrasts sharply with the severity of the decoration of the lower walls.

The treatment of the oval women's gallery, completed in 1732, as the inscription on the façade records, bears a close enough resemblance to the treatment of similar spaces in contemporary palaces and villas, in ballrooms and music rooms: there are comparable galleries in the Villa Widmann-Foscari and the Villa Foscari, on the Brenta Canal. Eighteenth-century churches and chapels were frequently built with musical performances in mind. One of the best-known examples is the Chiesa della Pietà, designed by Giorgio Massari at about the same time; his treatment of the choir stalls is similar to the treatment of the women's gallery in the Scuola Tedesca.

No written information exists, nor has any oral tradition survived, about the men who built the Scuola Grande Tedesca. But it is certain that they were local artisans accustomed to working in churches, schools, palaces and theatres; the profession of artist or artisan was not one of those permitted to the Jewish population of the Serenissima. Because of the outcry that would have arisen immediately from the Venetian artists' guilds, a Jewish artisan could never have opened his own workshop in the city.

One interesting exception to these restrictive rules throws light on the entrepreneurial stance adopted by the government in its dealings with the Jewish community. As early as the beginning of the seventeenth century the Senate granted them the right to set up any industry in the State of Venice provided it did not offer any competition to industries already in existence. In 1613 a certain Daniel Guastalla, a Paduan, was granted permission to sell a medicinal oil that he had discovered. In 1630 Namhan Judah, a Levantine Jew living in Venice, was licensed to manufacture cinnabar, sublimates and other chemical compounds used in the preparation of colours; he was also given permission to live outside the Ghetto, if this were necessary for his trade.

In the Tedesca synagogue, as in the Chiesa della Pietà and the Ospedaletto, a fine mesh hides the women from view; in the two churches, however, the women played an active part in proceedings, either as musicians or singers hidden from the public gaze. They were predominantly young orphans who had been given a home and educated by charitable institutions. Here in the synagogue the women are mere spectators who are not supposed to see what is going on in the room below: the men are praying, preaching, taking turns to read the sacred texts, singing or simply talking to one another. In the Jewish religion women perform an important task as educators, handing down the traditions of the faith to their families; outside the home however they are definitely second-class citizens. It is the men who take the lead in social and religious life, the men who have access to the sacred texts and are therefore in a position to lead the prayer in the synagogue. The reading of the Torah, or the recital of certain prayers, requires the presence of a minimum congregation of ten men; the presence of women in the synagogue is optional at all times.

It is not known what the earlier women's gallery in the Scuola Tedesca was like. It was probably a balcony fixed to one of the side walls. The eighteenth-century addition of a raised, oval gallery gave the room the harmony it lacked, and may also have improved the acoustics. According to David Cassuto, a historian of the Scuole, it is not impossible that the idea was copied from the Scuola Grande Spagnola, the largest of the Scuole in the Ghetto, where the women's gallery is an elliptical structure designed in the mid-seventeenth century by someone connected with the studio of Longhena. In the Scuola Spagnola, as in the Scuola Tedesca, there are obvious references to Venetian theatres of the day. In the Tedesca synagogue the impression of being in a theatre is increased by the ceiling, repainted in 1860 with *trompe l'oeil* geometric designs in blue and grey mosaic, surrounded by larger, oriental patterns. This is 'poor' (or inexpensive) decoration which looks as if it were temporary; in fact it has the same air of impermanence as theatrical design.

Jewish masks. Museo Civico Correr, Venice.

The Jews of the Ghetto shared the Venetian passion for music and the theatre. The Campo del Ghetto Nuovo was often used for the performance of plays which Christians as well as Jews were interested to see. Particularly during the festival of Purim, when everyone dons a disguise and dances in the streets (as at Carnival), people from outside the Ghetto would defy the ban that prohibited them from remaining in the Ghetto beyond a certain hour. Records exist of a comedy entitled *Esther*, by Salomon Usque, written in 1531, which was a great success and was revived several times. In the early seventeenth century a certain 'Rachel, the Jewish singer' was in demand in the salons of Venice, with her brother and her father; at the same period the famous Leon da Modena, cultural leader of the Ghetto, wrote the pastoral drama *Rachel and Jacob*. Often enough these plays had nothing Jewish about them except for the religion of their author. During Carnival time the Jews, tempted by the gaiety of Venetian life, would linger outside the Ghetto walls until late at night, as Salvator Silva, tried for the offence, records: 'It was the hour when the theatres begin to open, and when masks are put on. To my young age can be attributed my decision to go to the play'.

A final glance at the unusual interior of the synagogue leads to the following conclusions: the sense of sobriety provided by the classical benches and the severe, simple decoration of the walls is in sharp contrast to the frivolous elegance of the *bimah* and the women's gallery, the last two being redolent of seventeenth-century Venice. The contrast is sharp but never strident. A series of details draws the eye from one feature to the next, and gives rhythm and harmony to the whole. The geometrical designs on the wall panels are repeated in the decorations at the base of the *bimah*, on the parapet of the women's gallery and again in the *trompe l'oeil* mosaic on the ceiling. The sinuous lines of the feet of the benches recur in the cornucopias in the tympana above the Ark and the entrance door. The dense arabesques of the door of the Ark are echoed in the Art Nouveau grille covering the women's gallery. The colours of the interior provide a further unifying element; the warm wood tones and the gold are not dulled or chilled by the blue of the ceiling. Light from the branching lamps, and reflections from the canal below, make the rich gilding gleam and glow.

The Scuola Grande Tedesca is seldom used nowadays. Occasionally a member of the Jewish community in Venice, or a visitor, will ask to use it for a wedding or for some other special function. It ceased to be in regular use in October 1917, when the Jewish community was forced to disband. It was not possible, after the First World War, to resume regular worship. Administration of the various Scuole was taken over by a single body, the 'Templi Israelitici Riuniti'. The most recent restoration of the synagogue took place between 1975 and 1979; this was undertaken by the Comitato per il Centro Storico Ebraico of Venice, with the co-operation of the Comitato Italiano per Venezia and the Deutscher Koordinierungsrat, Frankfurt. The building was in a rather precarious state: the ceilings were sagging perceptibly, either because the load-bearing walls were giving way or because of earlier repairs and alterations to the roof. The roof joists were in a bad state of decay, some superfluous beams not having been removed at the appropriate time. The trusses of the beams and the masonry were unsafe, and so the women's gallery was closed to visitors. Rainwater pouring in had damaged both the woodwork and the masonry. The roof was repaired first, since this was the main cause of decay. The rotten trusses were removed and replaced, the roof was re-tiled and stone guttering was added. On the side of the Campo the outside wall at ground level was removed, lined with bitumen and rebuilt. The women's gallery was strengthened, and the Venetian floor of the main room, broken in several places, was restored. The woodwork was given preventive treatment against woodworm and rot, and all the gilding was cleaned and retouched.

THE SCUOLA CANTON

The Scuola Canton differs from the other synagogues in having its main façade along the Rio and its *bimah* on the southern corner of the Campo del Ghetto Nuovo. The little cupola just visible among the rooftops of the houses gives unmistakable charm to the building.

The little inscription beside the entrance of the Scuola Canton reads: 'Many are the wrongdoers, but whomsoever trusts in the Lord shall be surrounded by mercy' (*Psalms*, XXXII, 10.10).

Returning to the Campo del Ghetto Nuovo and looking again at the corner where the Scuola Grande Tedesca is situated, only a few metres farther on to the right is one of the strangest yet most typical buildings in the whole of the Ghetto: a small cubic structure, on the third floor, made of wood and topped by a curious octagonal lantern with an umbrella-shaped cupola, the whole looking slightly unsafe. This eccentric excrescence signals the presence of another 'special' building, another Scuola, just visible amongst a chaotic muddle of windows of all shapes and sizes, roofs, little balconies, and, sometimes, lines of washing hung out to dry.

A simple doorway, right beside the doorway of the Tedesca synagogue, bears the inscription: 'Constructed in 5292 (1532), the Synagogue of the Sacred Community of Canton'. Another stone, so worn by the rain as to be almost illegible, is built into the wall beside the doorway, near the present offices of the Jewish community. It reads: 'Much ill will befall the wicked, but he who puts his faith in God is surrounded by compassion' (from the *Psalms*).

The Scuola Canton is the second synagogue in the Ghetto and was built only four years after the nearby Scuola Tedesca. The reasons for building it are uncertain: it may have been because the community was growing, or, more probably, a group of people using the Tedesca synagogue may have wanted to break away and build a new place of worship. We know that the liturgy in use in the Scuola Canton at the beginning of this century was slightly different from the one in use in the Scuola Tedesca: a particular hymn was sung in the Scuola Canton ('Lechà dodi') which was not used next door. It was common amongst Jews of French origin to intone this hymn on the eve of the Sabbath. This and other details have convinced many scholars that the Scuola Canton was built by a group of French Ashkenazi Jews. The internal organization of the synagogue – this was the first of the Scuole in Venice to be built with the Ark and the *bimah* on opposite sides – supports this theory. At Carpentras and Cavaillon in the south of France, synagogues exist which are designed on these lines; it is a very unusual arrangement, however, found only very infrequently in European synagogues. It is therefore quite likely that the Scuola Canton was built by a group of Provençal Jews who wanted to maintain their traditional customs.

The curious name Canton also needs some explanation. The other four Scuole are all called simply by the origin of their owners: Tedesca, Italiana, Levantina and Ponentina. An obvious explanation, and one that is not too far-fetched, strikes anyone who looks at the synagogue from outside. In the Venetian dialect the word *canton* means corner, and this synagogue is set apart in a secluded corner of the Campo.

Another quite plausible solution may be that the name Canton, or Cantoni, was the name of the family, or group of related families, who financed the building of the new synagogue; Cantoni is still quite a common Jewish surname throughout Italy. In support of this hypothesis, there are still at least three small prayer rooms in the Ghetto Nuovo, which are privately owned synagogues bearing the names of the families who founded them (Scuola Luzzatto, Scuola Coanim and Scuola Meshullamim). So there would be nothing particularly unusual about the fact that the Scuola Canton possibly began life as a private prayer chamber, only later passing into the possession of the community. An added complication, however, is the existence of an ancient map, published by N. de Fer in Paris in the seventeenth century, which refers to the Ghetto as the 'Canton des Juifs'. Which of these three possible origins of the name 'Canton' is the correct one remains a mystery.

The stairwell of the Scuola Canton is lined with nineteenth-century memorial slabs in Italian and Hebrew, commemorating worthy members of the brotherhood of Canton.

The entrance to the Scuola Canton owes its elegance and size to the rebuilding work carried out in 1856. Recent strengthening work was subsidized by a number of committees in Italy and abroad.

The entrance and staircase to the synagogue were restored in 1859. The spacious, well-lit hall is divided by two white columns. Plaques on the wall beside the stairs record prominent members of the community: benefactors, preachers, rabbis, and so on. There are several doorways leading off the staircase, and one of these, on the first floor, now communicates directly with the Museum of Jewish Art.

The interior of the Scuola Canton is a regular rectangle, perhaps the most elegant of the Venetian synagogues in shape. Its present appearance owes much to successive rebuilding works during the eighteenth century.

Access to the synagogue is along a narrow corridor, with long benches against the sides. Four windows, curtained in red, and an elegant inlaid door connect the corridor with the main room. What was the exact function of this kind of antechamber? It is a long and very narrow space about 5 feet (1.5 metres) wide and it is unlikely that it could have been used for special ceremonies. The fact that the four windows overlook the main room lends credibility to the theory that this was originally the women's gallery. An inscription inside the synagogue draws our attention to the fact that the present women's gallery, a long gallery built above the entrance door and thus above the outer corridor, was erected in 1736. It is possible to conclude, therefore, that from the foundation of the synagogue in 1532 until 1736 women were confined to the antechamber and were 'sent upstairs' only after the rebuilding in the seventeenth century.

The four internal windows were only recently reopened (in 1980), in an attempt to restore the synagogue to its original appearance, having been bricked up in 1847. It is thought that during the period between 1736 and 1847 the corridor was used by poorer people who could not afford a seat in the synagogue and by those unable to find anywhere to sit down inside. The number of places was strictly limited, and it was something of a status symbol to own one: they were considered to be the personal property of their occupants and could be handed down from father to son.

Above the first door, at the entrance to the corridor, a plaque bears the same text in Hebrew and in Italian. It is by Joab Fano and is to be found in the Scuola Tedesca as well:

> Shrug off, oh man, all wicked thoughts
> As you go to pray in the temple.
> Focus your mind with ardent faith
> On the Divine Subject of your prayers.

This inscription, low down to the left of the *bimah*, records the gift by a private individual of 180 ducats, in 1532, for the construction of the synagogue.

Over the entrance to the synagogue itself a proverb from the Book of Solomon enjoins: 'Blessed is he who hears me, who diligently comes to my door every day'.

An elegant double door in the middle of one of the walls of the corridor leads into the synagogue. From the door the visitor will be struck, particularly on a sunny day, by the symmetry of the interior and the beautiful way it is illuminated. Natural light pours in through the five large windows looking over the canal, through the little coloured window over the *aaron* on the left, and through the little cupola over the *bimah* on the right. The room gives a feeling of order, with the various different elements merging into a consistent whole. The surprising tricks of perspective found in the Scuola Tedesca are absent here; instead there is an evident attempt at equilibrium and deliberate elegance.

The ground plan is a regular rectangle, very slightly and imperceptibly asymmetrical (42 x 23 x 41 x 21 feet/12.9 x 7.1 x 12.7 x 6.5 metres). The irregularity is so slight that it is not noticeable (unlike in the Scuola Tedesca), and the architects were not obliged to have recourse to any bold measures to counteract it. The eye is drawn to two elaborate structures on the left and on the right, which were built at an interval of almost a century, but which match one another perfectly.

The Ark, situated in the south-east of the Scuola as usual, bears a strong resemblance to the Ark in the other Ashkenazi synagogue, but it is even more richly decorated (if that is possible), and more distinguished. It is in three parts, with the niche for the Scrolls of the Torah in the centre at the top of four steps and the seats for the *parnassim* on either side. The tympanum over the Ark has a small window let into it; the window has fan designs in red, yellow and blue glass. It is supported by two fluted Corinthian columns and two pillars inlaid with oriental patterns in bas-relief. The decoration on the curved backs of the seats resembles the decoration on the door of the Ark, and it is finer and more elaborate than the work found in the Scuola Tedesca. Even the little columns that hold up the backs of the seats are sophisticated: the oblique fluting at the base contrasts with the vertical fluting of the upper part. The delicate flower patterns, repeated on all three parts, follow the rhythm of the columns, giving greater consistency to the whole than is to be found on the 'twin' in the Scuola Tedesca. The light filtering through the window above the tympanum provides a typically baroque effect; it gives vitality and interesting *chiaroscuro* touches to the Ark, which is almost in the shadows. The overall impression is perhaps of a less stately structure than the Ark in the Tedesca synagogue, but here more attention has been given to details of colour and design.

The two inscriptions visible above the seats are taken from the text of two Sabbath prayers; they are decorative as well as edifying. Another inscription, on the marble steps in front of the Ark, is interesting if obscure; it mentions a date which is probably that of the construction of

The Ark in the Scuola Canton shares many characteristics with the Ark in the nearby Scuola Tedesca. The woodcarving is more delicate here and the light effects more studied: it is altogether a more sophisticated piece of work.

the Ark: 'The gift of Joshua Moshe in memory of his brother who was slaughtered like a goat. The day of his birth was a difficult day for him. On his 44th birthday (44 = blood in the cabalistic system) his blood may be offered as a sacrifice to God. Mordechai, son of Menachem Baldosa, 1672.'

A date, 1736, and the names of the men responsible for restoring the synagogue are written above the entrance. This was the most thorough restoration the synagogue was to receive, and at this time the floor and the ceiling were rebuilt, the walls re-panelled, various items were gilded and the women's gallery was created on the upper floor.

The floor is the usual Venetian paving, with a central rosette and geometric patterns. The ceiling was painted dark blue in the nineteenth century, with stars scattered all over it and swags around the edge. During recent restoration the original white marbled ceiling has been revealed; a simple cornice in stucco is its only ornamentation. The handsome eighteenth-century lamps have also been recently restored.

The two side walls are remarkable for their large windows: the outside wall, on the canal, has five, and these are mirrored in the opposite wall by the door and the four windows connecting this room with the narrow corridor that gives access to the synagogue. Groups of five are to be found everywhere in this room – a clear reference to the five books of the Torah. The south-eastern wall, where the *aaron* is

Along the two side walls of the Canton synagogue are eight wooden bas-relief medallions containing tempera paintings of biblical scenes. Here the hailstorm of rocks is represented with naive realism.

A vision of Jerusalem with its cupolas and minarets echoes the cupolas and campaniles of Venice.

installed, is divided horizontally and vertically into twenty-five irregular panels. Similarly, the two longer walls are divided horizontally into five bands of different heights. Five steps lead up to the *bimah*. The importance of the number five in the external appearance of the three synagogues of the Ghetto Nuovo has already been noted; each has five windows on its façade.

A bench with a carved walnut backrest runs right round the walls; the design of the backrest is livelier than the similar one in the Scuola Tedesca. This one was probably the inspiration for the wall decoration in the nearby Scuola Italiana, built a few years later.

A richly carved and gilded wooden frieze runs along the wall above the windows. The large quantity of gilding in the two Ashkenazi synagogues demonstrates respect for the biblical precept which, on the subject of the Ark of the Covenant, says: 'And thou shalt gild it inside and out, and make golden garlands to hang around it' (*Exodus*, 37:2). More probably the current fashion in Venice for plasterwork and gilt was simply reflected in the synagogue. The Scuola Canton is unique among the Venetian synagogues in its eight relief medallions, in the frieze over the windows, painted in tempera, representing some of the most important biblical landscapes: Jerusalem, the Red Sea, the sacrificial altar, the manna in the wilderness, Noah's Ark, Moses drawing water from a stone, the falling of the hailstones and the River Jordan.

Landscapes are very rarely to be found in synagogues, and these probably derive from Central-European models. It is more common to find landscapes on fabrics than on the walls, such as on the curtain used to cover the Ark (some examples of these can be found in the Museum of Jewish Art nearby). The medallions in the frieze are somewhat primitive and of no great artistic merit but their interest lies in their rarity.

The women's gallery can be seen above the entrance, screened by dense gilded mesh in an aureole design. The same kind of design is repeated all round the room, which contributes to the overall harmony of the room and renders the area reserved for women almost invisible. The wall decorations are beautifully balanced, rich without being heavy. The sole interruption to their horizontal rhythm is a handsome classical doorway, with a draped marble pediment bearing a showy inscription.

The *bimah* of the Scuola Canton, which dates from about 1780, is constructed in a raised position, five steps high, inside a semi-hexagonal alcove three metres (nearly ten feet) deep. Light pours over the *bimah*, from the side as well as from above, through the small cupola that is visible from outside. The idea of a polygonal niche, jutting out – we shall encounter it again in other Venetian synagogues – is borrowed from a characteristic feature of Venetian domestic architecture, the so-called '*liagò*', a type of small covered loggia derived from Arabian models. The most original example is to be found in the Scuola Levantina in the Ghetto Vecchio.

Although it is opulently gilded and covered in plasterwork the *bimah* does not seem heavy, perhaps because it is modest in size. It calls to mind the rococo grace of certain drawing-rooms and boudoirs in Venetian palaces of the same period, for example, the Ridotto Venier, by the Ponte dei Bareteri, or the restored boudoir in Ca'Rezzonico. The exuberance of the ornamentation is modified by the delicacy of the colours and the lightness of the architectural details.

In the centre of the structure, detached from the rest, is a small gilded pulpit, polygonal, with a semi-elliptical arch over it, the vault of the arch being stuccoed in the softest green; it bears a strong resemblance to a stage. There are four small gilded columns, intertwined and pierced like climbing plants, two on each side. These are perhaps the most outstanding items in this synagogue, conferring it with an almost feminine grace. Inside the small apse the beautifully made chairs are reserved for prominent members of the community. A central alcove holds a shell-shaped basin, donated by Benjamin Marina de Consiglio, reminiscent of the carved wooden decoration in the choir stalls of fifteenth-century Venetian churches such as the Frari, or S. Zaccaria.

The *bimah* of the Scuola Canton was restored in about 1780 and then again in 1804. The four barley-sugar wooden columns, with their vines and bunches of grapes, and the natural light from above playing on the mouldings give a refined elegance to the whole.

Detail of the *bimah*. Four spiral columns in gilded wood flank a curved arch over the pulpit of the officiating elder. The columns consist of intertwined vines and bunches of grapes, reminiscent of the columns supporting the canopy in the Scuola Levantina (the latter are larger). Both draw their inspiration from the columns of the atrium in the Temple of Solomon. The restoration of the columns entailed cleaning and strengthening the wood, and scraping off unsightly bulges caused by the rusting of the nails; the wood was also treated against rot.

On either side of the apse there is a small window with leaded lights in geometric patterns. The cupola, above the pulpit, also has leaded lights, through which the daylight shines down on the prayer leader, adding weight and significance to his words. Low down on the left-hand wall of the *bimah* a stone plaque records the gift of 180 ducats by one Shelomo for the building of the synagogue in 1532.

The Canton synagogue was reopened to the public in 1989 after a long period of closure while restoration work was carried out. Work began in 1968, under the aegis of the World Monuments Fund and the Ministero per Beni Culturali e Ambientali. The first phase of the restoration was devoted to reroofing the building and restoring the ceilings and the floors. In 1973 a second phase of building work saw the partial rebuilding of the masonry, and the insertion of bands of reinforced concrete into the walls at ground level and on the first floor; this was carried out before any repairs were done to the foundations, to prevent the building from collapsing.

A grant from the Venice Committee in 1976 made it possible to cure the rising damp in the ground and first floors, thus removing a major threat to the synagogue. In 1979–80 further work was done to the roof and to the gilding. Next, the eighteenth-century lamps and the intertwining columns were restored, and missing woodwork was replaced. The complicated job of restoring and conserving the plasterwork in the cupola was successfully carried out, cleaning away the grime of centuries to reveal the original marbling. The step to the pulpit was also replaced.

After twenty years of work the Scuola Canton has regained its composure. Its charm is typically eighteenth-century: elegant surface decoration, delicate and harmonious colours, mostly pastel shades, and gilding. The atmosphere inside this casket is precious, but never excessively so; it transports us back in time to the century that was the most 'Venetian' of all.

An exterior view of the Scuola Canton on the Rio del Ghetto Nuovo. The projecting oblong contains the Ark of the Covenant, always built facing Jerusalem. Restoration of this synagogue was finished in 1989.

LIFE IN THE CAMPO DEL GHETTO NUOVO

After the rarified atmosphere of the Scuola Canton, the Campo seems very down to earth. Nowadays it is quiet, animated at certain times of the year by tourists, from Italy and further afield. Most of the shops around the square, apart from a few small tourist shops and one or two artisans' workshops, are empty. In the past, however, the Campo must have been very busy: we know that in the eighteenth century there were at least sixty tailoring workshops here. The women of the Ghetto were famous for the quality of their mending; their repairs were said to be so neat as to be invisible. A manuscript in the Museo Correr records that the women of the Ghetto were often afflicted with eye trouble because of the long hours they spent mending in very poor light, and that a terrible smell, apparently issuing from the old fabrics, filled the streets of the area. Beside these workshops were three pawnshops, also known as 'paupers' banks', identified by the colours of the receipts they gave: Banco Rosso, Verde, Giallo.

Campo del Ghetto Nuovo: the Sotopòrtego del Banco Rosso.

Jewish art in Venice today: Gianfranco Penzo, painter on glass, has his workshop in the Campo del Ghetto Nuovo.

Under the low colonnade to the right of the *sotopòrtego* the sign of the 'Banco Rosso' can still be seen. The fact that one of the commonest Jewish expressions in Venetian local theatre was 'far moscon', or 'moscogn', i.e. to pawn something, says a lot about the importance of these banks to a whole section of the poorer population of the city. The expression is used, for example, in *Pantalone Bullo*, by B. Gioanelli (1688); the Jew Bedanna says: 'O ben vegnu sior Pantalon; Menachai, Menachai, vien da basso, che e vegnu sior Pantalon, per far moscon'. ('Oh, welcome, Signor Pantalone. Menachai, Menachai, come upstairs, Signor Pantalone has come to pawn something.') Also in one of Goldoni's intermezzi, *La Pelarina*, 1730: 'Son giudio, son poveromo, /De mosconi son perfetto, /Ma onorato galantomo, /La dimanda a tutto el ghetto'. ('I'm a Jew, a poor man, very good at taking pledges, but an honourable gentleman, ask anyone in the Ghetto.')

A winter picture of the Ghetto Nuovo. Three wells, all dating from before 1516, are adorned with bas reliefs depicting the three lions of Judah.

The Sotopòrtego del Banco Rosso, in the Campo del Ghetto Nuovo. The words 'Banco Rosso', and the number 2912, still refer to one of the three 'paupers' banks' managed by the German Jews right up to the collapse of the Venetian Republic.

Campo del Ghetto Nuovo: detail of the bas relief on one of the three well-heads. Earlier carvings were scraped off and replaced by the lions of Judah.

There are three wells in the Campo. The oldest of these, the one near the old people's home, is made of Istrian stone, the other two in Verona marble. All the wells pre-date the Jewish occupation of the quarter and it is likely that the decorative shields have been altered, the original designs having been scratched out to be replaced by three lions of Judah. The oldest shield is lozenge-shaped and the other two ogival. The carving of the shields and rosettes is fairly crude, and resembles work frequently found on Venetian well-heads. It is unusual however to find three wells in the same square, but this was probably attributable to the heavy demand for water in a very crowded area.

The Holocaust Memorial, by the Lithuanian artist Arbit Blatas, was erected in 1980 near the Casa di Riposo.

THE SCUOLA ITALIANA

The façade of the Scuola Italiana, the third and last of the synagogues of the Ghetto Nuovo, can be seen facing towards the Ghetto Vecchio, just after the Scuola Canton. An unusual little addition to the outside, not found in any of the other Venetian synagogues, makes this one easily identifiable; this addition looks like a small temple built against the main wall, and it provides an elegant entrance porch to the synagogue. It is a brick structure containing private dwellings and two unremarkable balconies flank it on either side. It is supported by two columns and two pilasters in white stone. Above the porch, on the second floor, the five large windows of the synagogue can be seen, following the tradition which has already been discussed in the description of the other two Scuole in the Ghetto Nuovo. A careful look at the first floor, just to the left of the porch, in the places where the plaster has fallen off, reveals a further five slightly smaller arched windows, two of them bricked up. It is quite possible that this was another, smaller synagogue which may have fallen into disuse when the new one was built.

We know that the Scuola Italiana was founded in 1575; once again it is recorded in an inscription on the façade. The Italian Jews, with the *todeschi*, or German Jews, were the first to be confined to the Ghetto, as early as the beginning of 1516. It is reasonable to wonder why they allowed so much time to pass before building their own prayer and meeting room, when, as has already been described, the Scuola Tedesca had already been built in 1528, and the Scuola Canton only four years later. A possible answer is that they may have initially built a tiny prayer room, only about a quarter of the size of the present one, and only later managed to erect a larger and more prestigious hall.

This conjecture is not supported, however, by the existing access to the Scuola, which is up a dark and very steep staircase (traces of sixteenth-century paving can be seen on the landings), well to the left of the dignified portico designed as the entrance to the synagogue. It is possible that this staircase, which also gives access to some of the private dwellings, was built for the original synagogue, and that it was not until the opening of the later synagogue in 1575 that the decision was taken to construct a new staircase, this time directly beneath the portico. Nothing remains of this main staircase, and the portico has lost any function it may have had as a grand entrance to the synagogue, thereby in practice losing its connection with the synagogue.

The idea of an entrance porch in the shape of a classical temple must have come from the sixteenth-century synagogues of Rome, all destroyed at the end of the nineteenth century. These echoed the architecture of ancient Rome, and porches similar to the one on the Scuola Italiana were common. Only a few bad photographs and prints

Campo del Ghetto Nuovo: the exterior of the Scuola Italiana, with its characteristic portico, inspired by Roman architecture.

have come down to us, so it is not easy to make a direct comparison. The Jews of central Italy have also made an original contribution to the culture of their adopted country by importing architectural details from their own traditions, German, French or Provençal.

This community, made up of Jews from southern Italy, and above all from Rome (which possesses the oldest Jewish community in Italy), began its gradual movement northwards at the end of the thirteenth century, after a period of persecution which peaked in 1322 when the Talmuds were destroyed. They moved in small groups, sometimes single families at a time. Working for the most part as moneylenders, they finally intermingled with the community of northern Jews in the Veneto. In spite of differences in their tradition and liturgy, the Italian Jews in Venice never managed to escape being associated with the *Nazione*

The small eighteenth-century cupola over the *bimah* of the Scuola Italiana can be spotted from the centre of the Campo. Destroyed by fire in 1987, it has been faithfully rebuilt. The lower storeys are still inhabited and the staircase that leads to the synagogue also leads to the private apartments. As synagogues and private houses are mixed indiscriminately, it is quite possible to have a close-up view of the Scuola Italiana from the privacy of your terrace.

Above the windows of the Scuola Italiana a small plaque records the fact that the building of the synagogue was finished by the 'blessed Italian community in 1575'.

Todesca, and never succeeded in setting up on their own. But although they shared in all the activities of the German Jews they always remained a 'minority' group, both numerically and economically; they carried greater weight in religious and cultural life.

The façade of the Scuola Italiana bears the date of its foundation on a small shield above the central window, and the customary plaque (below the line of windows) also recalls the destruction of the Temple in Jerusalem.

At the top of the steep staircase is a compact entrance hall, panelled in wood, with a fairly low ceiling; the hall is joined to the main room of the synagogue by a door and by four internal windows, as in the Scuola Canton. It is likely that this hall was also used originally as a women's gallery, until a gallery over the main room was built at a later date. It is

This inscription in the hall preceding the main chamber records restoration work carried out in 1739–40.

also possible that this small anteroom, known as the *palush* by the Central European Jews, may have been used for special ceremonies, attended by a limited number of people, or it may have served simply as an anteroom to the main synagogue. The entrance hall in the Scuola Canton has already been described, and it is not impossible that the Scuola Tedesca also may have had something similar before the rebuilding of the staircase.

In this small antechamber there is a basin for washing hands, a symbolic act of purification before entry to the synagogue, and a wooden offertory. The Hebrew word for 'charity', *sedaka*, also means justice. Acts of charity, or acts of justice, are fundamental to the Jewish religion as they are to Christianity. There was a close-knit network of charitable and aid organizations in the Ghetto, each with its own special function and its own name, some of the latter quite colourful: The Redemption of Slaves, Marriage for Maidens, Succour to those in Childbirth, etc. The headquarters of these organizations were scattered through rooms next to the various synagogues and they fulfilled a function for the Jewish community comparable to the function performed by the religious aid foundations, Scuole, to be found all over Venice.

A small room panelled entirely in wood, forms an antechamber to the synagogue itself. As in the Scuola Canton, a series of internal windows provide visual contact between the two rooms.

The interior of the Scuola Italiana is particularly well lit, thanks to five large windows giving on to the Campo del Ghetto Nuovo. The sober elegance of the furnishings and the brightness of the room make a pleasant atmosphere; this is perhaps the least-known of the Jewish places of worship in Venice.

It was not only the synagogues in Venice that were called 'Scuole' (or sometimes Scuole Grandi, as in the case of the Tedesca and the Spagnola). The synagogues, like the Christian Scuole, were composed of a group of members who, in response to their religion's precepts on charity, undertook to help each other and to help their neighbours as well. It was imperative, for example, to look after the sick and infirm, to assist with funerals, to find dowries for girls from poor families and to free co-religionists taken prisoner by the Turks. The word 'schule' was used to indicate the synagogue throughout Central Europe; it is a direct translation of the Greek 'Scole', which means a place where people meet together for a particular purpose.

Entrance to the synagogue is through a door in the centre of the wall. The room is virtually a square (33 x 30 feet/10 x 9.3 metres), and the *bimah* and the Ark can be seen immediately on entry. Seen from the door the Scuola Italiana looks different from the previous two synagogues, which were much longer. This room has a very high ceiling, so the impression is almost of a cube.

After the sumptuous furnishings and the rich gilding of the Scuola Tedesca and the Scuola Canton, this synagogue may be a disappointment. Sobriety and austerity are the words that best describe its interior. Here, as in the nearby Scuola Canton, the *bimah* and the Ark are opposite one another, but the effect is very different because of the shape of the room. The *bimah* dominates the scene, on account of its size (it almost constitutes a room on its own) and its elevation: it stands over four feet (1.4 metres) higher than the floor. The Ark here is not built in as it is in the other Scuole, and it does not bulge out on the outside. One novelty not found in the other two synagogues is a little wooden enclosure separating the Ark from the rest of the room.

Gold inscriptions on black stone run right round the walls; they are backed by pale-coloured stucco panels with relief patterns of rosettes and ribbons. The lower part of the wall is panelled (as in the other synagogues) with a high backrest made of wood, and a wooden bench runs right round the walls. The carving on the cherry-wood panels is similar to that in the Canton synagogue, with the same pattern of squares and curves. The five windows on to the Campo are proportionately much larger than those in the other Scuole, and the flood of light they admit brings the little interior to life in a particularly vivid way. Another source of light is the small cupola over the *bimah*; it resembles the cupola in the Scuola Canton in shape and size. At the present moment this umbrella-shaped cupola, visible from the centre of the Campo, is being restored after being destroyed by fire on 6 April 1988, during repair work to the roof of the building.

Dating the various elements inside the Scuola Italiana is a difficult task. We know that rebuilding work was undertaken in 1739–40, as a plaque giving this information is to be found in the entrance hall. Even though this was a period of decline for the Jews of the Venetian Ghetto, restoration and redecoration of the interior of the synagogues was carried out with the greatest care. The Scuola Grande Tedesca was rebuilt in 1732, the Scuola Canton in 1736, as has already been noted. The same passion for beauty and luxury was current in the rest of Venice, in spite of worsening political and economic instability, and many families spent a fortune on building and modernizing their palaces, or on donating a new façade to an old church.

The *bimah* can probably be ascribed to the mid-eighteenth century, when the rebuilding works were done; it is constructed at such a height that it appears detached from the rest of the room. Four Corinthian columns in wood rather than marble, on high bases, support a heavy stucco cornice which goes right round the room, diverging only to form twin arches over the *bimah* and the *aaron*; the arches underline the importance and the promixity of the two elements. The cornice may be one of the oldest items in the synagogue, and it is also one of the most impressive. The vault of the ceiling, exceptionally fine and now at last restored, is slightly curved like the keel of a ship; the ceiling is square in shape, with rounded corners, and repeats the pattern of the stucco cornice. The decoration of the *bimah* and the ceiling probably date from the mid-eighteenth century, and are the oldest remaining parts of the synagogue. The wooden bench also dates from that period.

Although the semi-octagonal *bimah* is separated from the room by eight steps, and is unusually large (nearly 10 feet/3 metres deep and 20 feet/6 metres wide), it matches the rest of the room because the pattern of three different-coloured bands found on the walls continues around its exterior. On the lower part, the same pattern of squares found in the room below is repeated on the bench and the bench back. The seats inside the *bimah* were reserved for the *parnassim*, or administrators, elected from the oldest and most influential members of the synagogue. The upper part bears a larger, very pale pink panel with a black stone plaque in the centre, on which are inscribed the duties of the precentor and advice on how he should behave towards the congregation. Similar plaques occur on the walls of the main room. The decoration of the lower walls probably dates from the rebuilding of 1739–40, while the stucco with the black inscribed stone plaques dates probably from the restoration of 1809. The inscription under the pulpit in the *bimah* refers to this early nineteenth-century restoration and it is similar to the one in the Scuola Canton, but much less highly decorated. The elegant script informs us that 'the tower in the house of Our Lord was renovated in the year 5569–1809'. So, to distinguish between changes made during the two different restorations, it is probable that the *bimah*, of eighteenth-century construction, was enriched in the early nineteenth century with stucco panels, a new pulpit and new decoration on the steps and the bases of the four columns.

The date of the women's gallery is uncertain; the simple grille of the gallery is visible above the entrance, access to the gallery being from the little anteroom up a steep wooden staircase. Its construction probably dates from the period 1739–40, when the synagogue was rebuilt; it is slightly later than the gallery in the Scuola Canton.

Scuola Italiana: the *bimah*, seen from the women's gallery. Established in 1575, and rebuilt subsequently several times, the Italian synagogue is the least ostentatious of the five public synagogues in the Venetian Ghetto.

The covering of the upper part of the walls of the room dates from 1810. This is the date mentioned in the inscription over the entrance, which reads:

Shining abode of God and light of our eyes,
Whose beauty and whose decoration were munificently given;
Several members of the community have given labour and money,
In order that this dwelling might delight us with its appearance, and with
  voices raised in prayer.
Oh Lord, help us to build this sanctuary as a monument to him who
  rests in the shadow of God. It was completed in the year 1809.

The name of the person dedicating the work can be found in the acrostic: it is Izhàk Norzi. The name of the dead man, obtained from the acrostic around the walls, is Abraham. All the inscriptions end with the word *shalom*, peace, the word traditionally used to end tomb inscriptions and the symbol of eternal peace.

The inscriptions on the wall are invocations to God. We know that until 1929 the walls of the Scuola Italiana were deocrated with thirteen leather bands, bearing almost incomprehensible inscriptions which may have come from another prayer room; they referred to the termination of a long period of grave sickness and disasters, possibly the end of the terrible plague of 1630.

The nineteenth-century inscriptions attempt to give more didactic force to the interior decoration of the Scuola. They also match the interior design: the light coloured plasterwork is in vivid contrast to the dark colour scheme used elsewhere in the room, and it certainly makes the general impression more cheerful.

The *aaron* (Ark) is a heavy piece of furniture from the early nineteenth century, a conscious imitation of the two more complex Arks in the other two synagogues in the Ghetto Vecchio. Besides the fact that it is made of wood, rather than of marble, it is also a much less fine piece of work. To illustrate this with an example: instead of real inlaid wood, this Ark is decorated with imitation inlay, made from pieces of wooden moulding glued to the surface. As a piece of work the Ark is much more modest, less pretentious than the contemporary *bimah*. The balustrade, with little columns and interlaced arches, common features of the furnishings of the day, was donated by Menachem Joshua Guglielmi in 1842.

Behind the *aaron*, completely hidden from view, is a tiny room, used nowadays as a store room. It was probably originally the alcove for the first *aaron*, which has not survived. Like the *bimah*, the *aaron* has an

Interior of the Scuola Italiana, looking towards the *bimah*. The airy, almost cubic chamber differs from the other, longer synagogues in the Ghetto because of its central plan. The furnishings, mainly from the eighteenth and nineteenth centuries, have been carefully restored.

The Ark of the Covenant, a heavy, nineteenth-century piece, is designed in conscious imitation of the monumental arks in the Scuola Spagnola and the Scuola Levantina; it fails, however, to achieve their artistic stature.

arch over it, which interrupts the continuity of the cornice; in addition the *aaron* has a heavy, velvet canopy over it, erected in the nineteenth century, similar to the one in the Scuola Spagnola. A handsome Dutch standard lamp completes the decoration of the Ark.

The overall effect, particularly since restoration work was finished, may not achieve the same scintillating elegance as the other two Scuole, but it is impressive nevertheless. Careful restoration of the ceiling, which entailed cleaning off the nineteenth-century paintings, has revealed plain white plasterwork which goes well with the stuccoed walls and also with the bright light pouring in from outside; it contrasts violently with the black wall panels and the gold inscriptions, and brings to life an interior which would otherwise be too sombre.

Back in the Campo once more, it is time to look at the most heavily restored part of the square, the side along the Canale di S. Girolamo. Here the dense wall of very tall buildings shrinks a little, and opens out to the outside world. In 1836 the existing buildings on this side were demolished and rebuilt in a lower, more rational style; the buildings were first used as a 'Casa d'Industria' (workshops), but were then turned into an old people's home (Casa di Riposo). To the right of the building, a cast-iron bridge links the little island of the Ghetto Nuovo to the Fondamenta degli Ormesini. This used to be one of the other entrances to the quarter; there are still two tiny buildings, on either side of the bridge, which used to be sentry boxes for the guards of the Ghetto.

Inside the Casa di Riposo, just to the right of the front door, there is a small prayer room which is still in use for special functions, usually private. Amongst the mostly eighteenth-century furnishings, the Ark is the most conspicuous with its simple, classical lines. It almost certainly came from the Scuola Meshullamim, one of the three private prayer and study rooms that used to exist in the Ghetto Nuovo.

The Scuola Meshullamim was established in about 1600 by a certain Mose Meshullam Levi. The only item of furniture remaining today is the Ark; the other two private Scuole were more fortunate. The Scuola Luzzatto and the Scuola Coanim, both established in the early seventeenth century, were relocated in the nineteenth century on the ground floor of, respectively, the Scuola Levantina and the Scuola Spagnola. They will be described later.

A plaque on the façade of the Casa di Riposo commemorates Giuseppe Jona, president of the Jewish Community of Venice, who, on 16 September 1943, when Venetian Jews were beginning to be rounded up and deported by the Nazis, committed suicide.

On the left-hand wall, seven bronze figures were erected on 25 April 1980 in memory of the victims of the Holocaust, given to the city by the Lithuanian sculptor and painter Arbit Blatas. Persecution of the Jews in Venice by the Fascist and Nazi regimes accounted for the lives of nearly two hundred people. There were two very determined manhunts, the first on the night of 5–6 December 1943, when about a hundred people were arrested and sent to the concentration camp at Fossoli, later to be deported to Germany when the camp came under Nazi control. Then in the summer of 1944 there were several raids, in one of which twenty-two people were taken from the old people's home, and twenty-nine from the hospital; amongst the latter was the octogenarian Chief Rabbi, Adolfo Ottolenghi.

One of the seven bronze panels that forms part of the Holocaust Memorial, given by Blatas to Venice in 1980.

The Casa di Riposo Israelitica, or Jewish rest home, founded in the last century, housed about twenty people. The side of the Campo where it is situated has been totally rebuilt since 1836.

THE GHETTO VECCHIO

The Ghetto Nuovo and the Ghetto Vecchio are linked by a little bridge on the Rio degli Agudi. The erstwhile foundry area, the Ghetto Vecchio, was conceded to the Levantine Jews, hitherto squashed into the crowded Ghetto Nuovo, in 1541. Later, officially in 1589 but in practice certainly earlier, the concession was extended to the Ponentine Jews, Jews of Iberian origin, who had just arrived.

The new sector was given an artificial boundary when a wall was built towards the Rio di Cannaregio, and towards the other sides; even the side looking towards the Ghetto Nuovo, along the Rio degli Agudi, was blocked off, depriving the quarter of any access to the water's edge. To isolate the area even more completely the windows facing the outside were walled up, as were any doors of neighbouring Christians that opened on to the Ghetto.

The gate that had originally barred the way between the old and new Ghettos disappeared, but this did not signify that the two areas were united. Legally they remained autonomous, under the control of two different magistratures. The 'Todeschi' came under the Magistratura del Cattaver, the Levantines and the Ponentines under that of the Cinque Savi alla Mercanzia.

Day began early in the Ghetto, often before dawn, with the opening of the gates, guarded by Christian sentries. Then the inhabitants were called by a knock on the door to hasten to the synagogue for morning prayers. As soon as prayers had begun a last warning was given to late-comers with trumpet blasts throughout the quarter. The Ghetto Nuovo was always more visited by Christian 'outsiders' than the Ghetto Vecchio, because that is where the pawnshops and the old clothes dealers plied their trade. The Ghetto Vecchio, on the other hand, was occupied by international merchants rather than small business folk, and it was calmer and more secluded from the bustle of the city. The main street, then called the 'strada maestra', now the Calle del Ghetto Vecchio, contained shops used mainly by the inhabitants of the quarter: the baker, the kosher butcher, the greengrocer, etc. There was also a hospital and an inn. The Ghetto Nuovo was known by the poor all over Venice for its specialized shops, the pawnshops and the old clothes shops; the Ghetto Vecchio, apart from the unusual height of some of its buildings, was more integrated into the city of Venice itself. This is still obvious today if you study the street plan of the area (see p. 172). It is not an island, like a fortress surrounded by a moat, in the way the Ghetto Nuovo is. A long street, at the end of which a small Campo is visible, is crossed at several intersections of its length by smaller streets – a very typical Venetian cityscape. The inhabitants of the Ghetto Vecchio, like many other Venetians, would leave their quarter every morning to go to work near

The Calle del Ghetto Vecchio. Known previously as the Strada Maestra (High Street), this *calle* closely resembles others in the city of Venice.

At the far end of the Ghetto Vecchio, just before emerging into the Fondamenta di Cannaregio, the lane narrows. While urgent repairs are awaited, a highly visible prop supports the precarious buildings.

Ghetto Vecchio: Calle dell'Orto. The name records the presence of small plots of land, traces of which can still be seen today.

Little known by visitors to the Ghetto, but no less interesting for that, the Calle and the Corte dell'Orto are reached (if you are coming from the Ghetto Nuovo) from the lefthand side of the bridge.

the Rialto, the business centre of the city, and they would often be absent abroad on business trips. It is obvious that their experience of Ghetto life was very different from that of the inhabitants of the Ghetto Nuovo, who spent most of their working life within the suffocating walls of the Campo.

While walking through the Ghetto Vecchio it is interesting to look at the names of the *calli* and the small courtyards. Immediately on your right is a Calle Barucchi, now closed. Further along, beyond the little Campo with the well, is a Corte Rodriga. As is often the case in Venice, these lateral streets were called after the family living in them, an indication that these were important, well-known families. There is nothing comparable in the Ghetto Nuovo, where the anonymous tenement blocks do not invite such familiarity, as modern tower blocks on the outskirts of a city repel individuality even today.

Other names indicate the particular use an area was put to: left of the little bridge is a Calle dell'Orto, leading to a Corte dell'Orto, where there is still a huge garden. In spite of the density of the population of the Ghetto Vecchio it was still possible to find some land to cultivate; this was typical of the Cannaregio area as well, well provided in those days with gardens and vegetable plots which have only been built on relatively recently to house the growing population.

On the way to the Campiello delle Scuole, originally called the Campiello del Pozzo, a broad opening on the right leads to two parallel *calli*, Calle Sporca and Calle del Forno. Calle Sporca, still worthy of its name (Dirty Lane), is a narrow passage between two very tall buildings like skyscrapers which dominate the whole of the Ghetto Vecchio: even the place where the Sephardic Jews were enclosed was isolated and overcrowded. According to photographic evidence, until the end of the nineteenth century these buildings were even higher, with two more storeys on top. The building at the back, away from the Campiello, was known as 'delle Scalematte' (of the crazy staircase), probably because of the twisting stairs joining the two buildings, forerunners of the dismal staircases in the tower blocks of today. It is preferable to climb up the building facing the Campiello; even today the stairs are entirely made of wood.

Details of a doorway in the Calle del Ghetto Vecchio, near the Campiello delle Scuole.

The Calle Sporca in the Ghetto Vecchio, narrow and suffocating. The two tall dwellings were probably linked in former times by external staircases ('scale matte', or 'crazy stairs').

As in the Ghetto Nuovo, these two tall houses in the Ghetto Vecchio bear witness to the problems of housing that afflicted the population, particularly in the sixteenth and seventeenth centuries.

The narrow staircases of the multi-storey dwellings in the Ghetto Vecchio, constructed entirely of wood, twist and turn ever upwards, through at least seven storeys.

Ghetto Vecchio: Campiello delle Scuole, formerly called the Campiello del Pozzo. The two Sephardic synagogues face one another, surrounded by many private dwellings.

Besides the two 'skyscrapers' and the synagogues, there is one other building in the Ghetto Vecchio which is worthy of attention for its historical interest rather than for any intrinsic architectural merit. This is the '*midrash*' (a religious school devoted to the study of texts) of Leon da Modena, to be found half-way down the *calle* on the left, coming from the bridge. All that is to be seen is an arched door, more dignified than its neighbours, flanked by two arched windows, closed and barred: the structure resembles the Arks of the Covenant already examined in the Scuole of the Ghetto Nuovo.

Calle del Ghetto Vecchio, entrance to the midrash of Leon da Modena. Leon da Modena (1571–1648) was the most significant cultural figure in the Venetian Ghetto; the school of da Modena grew up quite close to the Levantine synagogue.

Jewish cemetery of San Nicolo del Lido, Venice. On the tombstone of Sara Copio Sullam (1592–1642), were inscribed these verses composed by her teacher, Leon da Modena:

This is the stone of the distinguished
Signora Sara, wife of the living
Jacobbe Sulam
The exterminating angel shot his dart,
    wounding Sara mortally
A lady of great intelligence
Wise among women
Supporting those in need
The poor found a companion and friend
    in her
Though now Sara lies defenceless against
    insects
On the appointed day the Good Lord
    will say: return, return, Oh Sulamita
She abandoned life on the 6th day of Adar
    by the Jewish calendar
May her soul enjoy eternal beatitude.

The Rabbi Leon da Modena (1571–1648) was the leading figure during one of the most flourishing periods in the history of the Ghetto, a relatively stable period when exchanges between the cultural leaders of the Jewish quarter and Venetian intellectuals were particularly intense and productive. Thanks to Leon da Modena, Hebrew typography in Venice, already well known at the time of Daniel Bomberg in the first half of the sixteenth century, received new stimulus. His efforts at interpreting Jewish tradition to the outside world were of fundamental importance: his *History of Jewish Ceremonies* was an important milestone. An eclectic, often contradictory character, he dedicated himself to teaching for twenty-five years. Tradition has it that his little school was in this modest building in the Ghetto Vecchio, a short distance from the Sephardic synagogues. Teaching, however, did not absorb all this mighty man's energies, and he says in his autobiography that he practised at least twenty-six professions. We encounter him as a successful preacher, tragedian, director of an academy of music, and incorrigible (but luckless) gambler.

Da Modena was certainly the most prominent man of his day, but some of his contemporaries are also worthy of note. One of the most important was, exceptionally enough, a woman, Sara Copio Sullam (1590?–1641), a friend of da Modena; she was a brilliant scholar of Hebrew and Latin, a poet, who presided over a literary salon to which all the brightest names in the Venetian cultural firmament used to come. Leon da Modena's most brilliant disciple was Simone Luzzatto, author of a *Discourse on the State of the Jews*, published in 1638, in which he estimates the influence of the Jewish community in Venice in political and economic terms.

Tombstone of Leon da Modena in the Jewish cemetery of San Nicolo del Lido, Venice.

THE SCUOLA GRANDE SPAGNOLA

The broad façade of the Scuola Grande Spagnola closes the Campiello delle Scuole at the far end. It is a simple, elegant, if somewhat severe façade, with a line of four large arched windows on the upper floor with leaded lights in a pattern of small circles. The windows are outlined in white stone, and each has a light corbel above it. The impression is unexciting and inconspicuous compared with the richly decorated façade of the Scuola Levantina, almost opposite. The lower floor contains various small windows, asymmetrically placed. The rooms below the synagogue were apparently used as study rooms in the old days, but now they are all private residences with their own front doors. Between the two floors a plaque commemorates the victims of the Holocaust.

On the right, near the corner, a massive wooden door, richly carved with floral patterns similar to those on the nearby Scuola Levantina, leads to the synagogue of the Ponentine Nation, commonly known as the Scuola Spagnola. The inscription over the door reads: 'Blessed are they who dwell in thy house and give thee everlasting praise' (from the Book of Psalms). This is the largest and best-known synagogue in Venice, and is still in regular use today by the Jewish community of Venice, reduced by now to little more than five hundred people. At present the two synagogues in the Ghetto Vecchio are used alternately; they are larger and easier of access than the synagogues in the Ghetto Nuovo. Each week, on Friday evening and Saturday morning, the Sabbath is celebrated here. (The new day begins at the rising of the first three stars on the preceding evening, which is why the Sabbath begins on a Friday evening.) In autumn and winter it is celebrated in the Scuola Levantina, at present the only synagogue with central heating, and in the Scuola Spagnola in spring and summer. The most important festivals are celebrated in the Scuola Spagnola: Pesach, the Jewish Easter, which celebrates the liberation of the Jews from slavery in Egypt and the crossing of the Red Sea, and then the three great celebrations at the beginning of autumn: Rosh Hashana (New Year), Yom Kippur (a day of fasting and expiation) and Sukkot (the festival of settlement). Other festivities are rarely celebrated nowadays: weddings and bar mitzvahs (the entry into adult male life at thirteen) and even concerts have all but disappeared.

When the Jews from different nations united in Venice the Scuola Spagnola became the official headquarters of the community. Tradition has it that this synagogue has the absolute right, above all others in the world, to remain in use from the day of its foundation for ever. Even before the reunification of the Jews this was always the leading synagogue in the Ghetto. Important delegations frequently made their way to the famous Venetian Jewish quarter, and they would be received in the Scuola Spagnola and entertained according to their rank.

Interior of the Scuola Grande Spagnola, looking towards the Ark. Parallel rows of benches bring together the two poles, the Ark and the *bimah*. Nowadays the women sit to the left of the door behind a simple wooden grille that separates them symbolically from the menfolk.

The two Sephardic synagogues in the Ghetto Vecchio, one opposite the other, occupy almost the entire area of the Campiello delle Scuole. Both were rebuilt in the seventeenth century and are still in regular use.

In 1629 the Duc d'Orléans, brother of the King of France, wanted to pay a visit to the Ghetto in the company of other civic authorities, plus a huge retinue. He was welcomed in the Scuola Spagnola on his arrival by a speech composed for the occasion by the ubiquitous Leon da Modena, already a very popular preacher whose sermons were attended by crowds of the nobility of Venice and even prelates of the church.

The entrance to the synagogue is a large, rectangular room with a bench running right round the walls; the lower part of the walls is panelled in wood, as in the other synagogues. Above the wooden backrest is a series of plaques commemorating the virtues of prominent local worthies and benefactors of the community. The oldest inscriptions, on the left, are written only in Hebrew; the ones on the right, dating from the nineteenth and twentieth centuries, are all translated into Italian. There is another plaque (on the right at the back) which records the year when the new staircase was built and the organ was introduced (1894).

On the wall at the back, between the two doors, a parchment bears the list of Venetian Jews deported and exterminated during the Nazi occupation. Above this list, on the wall, is an inscription in memory of Marco Voghera, a young Venetian who was killed in Israel in 1973, during the Yom Kippur war. The right-hand door leads to a small courtyard used during festivals. It is used as a 'hut' during the festival of Sukkot.

In the centre of the right-hand wall an elegant bronze gate closes the archway that leads to the staircase. The stairway branches into two, one for each door to the synagogue and the ceiling above the stairs is decorated with a *trompe l'oeil* caisson (a sunken panel in a flat or vaulted ceiling). To the left and right of the first flight are two beautiful inlaid doors. Originally these led to the offices of the Ponentine community whose headquarters were here; nowadays they are used to store candles, cloths and so on. It is curious that here, as in many of the palaces in Venice, the windows of the mezzanine open onto the hall; what little light these rooms receive comes from there. The reference to contemporary Venetian domestic architecture is obvious: the '*mezà*', or mezzanine floor, was used for utilities and sometimes as living quarters for the servants, the first floor, or '*piano nobile*', held the grand reception room, or '*pòrtego*'.

In this case the *piano nobile* houses the synagogue itself. The double access to the room is from either side of the *bimah*, which is edged with a heavy marble parapet. Anyone climbing the stairs to go into the synagogue remains hidden from those inside until the actual moment of entry into the huge room; the effect is definitely theatrical, like the sudden entry of an actor from the wings on to the stage. There are no doors, as there were in the other synagogues, nothing to separate it from the bustle of everyday life: the transition from the external world into the world of prayer and meditation and study is unmarked. The size of the room, at 42 x 69 feet (13 x 21 metres) much larger than any of the other Scuole in the Ghetto, makes an immediate impression, as does the richness and variety of the decoration. The Scuola Grande Spagnola is certainly the most grandiose of the Venetian synagogues, and the one most able to rival the size and opulence of the Christian churches nearby. The simplicity of the façade increases the surprise of visitors when they come upon such an explosion of opulence within.

The earliest instances of antisemitic persecution in the Iberian peninsula occurred at the end of the fourteenth century. The Dominicans were the leaders of violent attacks against the Jewish community, who had been peacefully established in Spain for centuries and who had made an important contribution to the cultural as well as the economic life of the peninsula. It eventually reached the stage when study of the Talmud was prohibited and Jews were forced into conversion. It is known that there were at least 190 synagogues in Spain at the beginning of the fourteenth century. But a century later many of them, including some magnificent ones like the two in Toledo and the Cordòba synagogues had had to be abandoned, or had sometimes been transformed into churches. Finally, in 1492, under the rule of Ferdinand of Aragon and Isabella of Castile, the Jews of Spain were ordered either to become Christians or, within the space of twenty four hours, to leave the country and find refuge elsewhere. A similar fate befell the Jews of Portugal, four years later.

Some left the country immediately, often making for the Ottoman Empire. But many others stayed, and accepted conversion. The *conversos*, or *cristianos nuevos* were always suspected, often quite rightly, of having accepted their new faith in appearance only. They were nicknamed, both in Spain and Portugal, *marrano*, or pig. Those accused of 'marranism' could be condemned to be burnt to death. Nevertheless there was a continuous flow of *marranos* into other parts of Europe throughout the whole sixteenth century; some went north, to Holland in particular, some to the Mediterranean ports. In Italy groups of *marranos* gathered in Rome, Florence, Ferrara and Ancona.

The *marranos*, merchants either by tradition or necessity, were attracted to Venice by the Rialto, an important centre of commerce, and also by the existence of a stable Jewish community within the city. The Serenissima reacted to their arrival with instinctive diffidence at first, either because of their religious ambiguity, or because they feared

A Sephardic tombstone in the Jewish cemetery of S. Nicolo del Lido: the symbol of the jug and bowl belongs to the Levi family.

economic competition. The newcomers were considered shrewd operators and reckless adventurers. In 1497, then again in 1550, Venice, under pressure from the church in Rome, expelled the *conversos*. However the refugees were by now there to stay; they were openly declaring themselves as Jews more and more frequently, and were making a favourable impact on the business life of the city. The Venetian Inquisition held about seventy trials against *giudazzanti*, people professing to be Jews, but in the majority of instances the cases were dismissed or, if the accused was found guilty, an extremely light sentence would be preferred.

A tombstone of a member of the Habib family, Sephardic in origin, in the Jewish cemetery of S. Nicolo del Lido. Many of these families, ennobled in Spain before their expulsion in 1492, continued to use their titles even when in exile.

The first synagogue on the site of the Scuola Spagnola was probably constructed in 1584, the date of the earliest reference to it in existing documents, five years before the famous order, and the present synagogue was rebuilt in the seventeenth century. Some scholars, including Ottolenghi and Pinkerfeld, have suggested earlier dates, but without any supporting documentary evidence.

It is known that the earlier synagogue was in the Campiello, and it must have been quite large if Leon da Modena's description of the visit of the Duc d'Orléans and his retinue in 1629 is anything to go by. Although almost nothing is known about the original appearance of the two Scuole in the Ghetto Vecchio, we do have a lively written description of some of the more frivolous aspects of life in the Ghetto at the beginning of the seventeenth century, a few years after the momentous order of 1589. Thomas Coryat, in his *Coryat's Crudities*, published in London in 1611, gives his impressions of his trip to Venice in 1607.

Coryat tells us that he saw, in the women's galleries of the synagogues of Venice:

> … many Jewish women, some of whom were more beautiful than any woman I have ever seen, and so elegant in their dress, adorned with gold chains and rings ornamented with precious stones, such that certain of our English countesses would have difficulty in rivalling. They wear wonderful long trains, like the trains worn by Princesses who have ladies' maids whose whole function is to look after them: this shows the great wealth of some of these Jews.

Coryat visited the Ghetto at the peak of its cultural and economic success. It was during this period of stability and well-being that the decision was taken to rebuild the synagogue of the Ponentine community, the present Scuola Grande Spagnola, destined to become the largest of the Scuole in the Jewish quarter of Venice and, as was mentioned before, to be uninterruptedly in use up to the present day.

An expert on art in seventeenth-century Venice, Elena Bassi, is of the opinion that the façade of the synagogue, with its white stone reliefs characteristic of the style of Longhena, the architect of S. Maria della Salute, probably dates from the fourth decade of the seventeenth century. The interior is probably about twenty years later. Cecil Roth, presumably quoting oral tradition, dates the construction as the year 1635. Unfortunately, neither documents nor inscriptions give the date of the foundation of either the Scuola Spagnola or the Scuola Levantina. The absence of this information reveals quite a different mentality from that

The elliptical women's gallery of the seventeenth-century Scuola Grande Spagnola has certain characteristics in common with Venetian theatres of the period. The gallery is no longer in use.

of the founders of the three synagogues in the Ghetto Nuovo, who were punctilious about recording the date of building and major rebuilding on plaques and inscriptions.

Art historians are generally agreed that the person responsible for building the Scuola belonged to the artistic entourage of Baldassare Longhena (1598–1682). Longhena dominated religious and civil architecture in Venice for a large portion of the seventeenth century, and he had a lasting influence on the generation of artists who succeeded him. The number of buildings designed by him in Venice is very large.

Interior of the Scuola Grande Spagnola, looking towards the Ark of the Covenant. Many-branched Dutch chandeliers, oil lamps and large candles light up the synagogue in theatrical fashion, giving warmth to the dark woodwork of the benches and the fiery red of the hangings.

Apart from a few buildings that bear his signature, the attribution of this large oeuvre is very difficult. Our synagogue comes into this category: did Longhena design the building and keep an eye on the building works, as tradition would have it, or, as some scholars have suggested, was the work carried out by one of his many pupils or followers?

The name of Antonio Gaspari (c.1630 to after 1730), one of Longhena's collaborators, has been cited in this context; the two worked together on important buildings such as the Palazzo Pesaro on the Grand Canal. Documents have come to light that prove that he received commissions from two Jewish clients in Venice. Another possibility is that the Ponentine Jews did what many others would do when they required a public building, and turned to a recognized architect whose work was admired by an influential member of the group. If this was the case then the synagogue must have been rebuilt much earlier than 1635 as proposed by Roth. On the other hand it was quite common in Venice for a particular design or style to be such a success that it was repeated for years, often decades, after its initial introduction, even though tastes might have changed in the meantime. This tendency to conserve styles is another reason why the attribution of an exact date to a building in Venice can be so problematic.

A stylistic detail typical of Longhena is the Ark of the Covenant, which catches the eye immediately at the far end of the room. A high blue arch, decorated with gold stars and an inscription, 'Know ye before Whom ye stand', surrounds a marble structure with a double tympanum; it bears a remarkable resemblance to many of the seventeenth-century altars in the churches of Venice.

The Ark itself occupies a rectangular alcove, quite small in size; the broad, semi-circular Ark, supported on columns, extends the rectangle. This type of structure, known as an *edicola*, harks back to designs of the Renaissance, and was a design not often used by Longhena. It can, however, be found in some of his later buildings, dating from between 1660 and 1670. The surprising similarity between the Ark in the Scuola Spagnola and the altar of the Cappella Vendramin in the church of S. Pietro di Castello, designed by Longhena in 1663, has been remarked upon. The central portion of the *edicola* is occupied by the Ark in the synagogue and by the altarpiece in the church (in the case of S. Pietro, a painting by Luca Giordano). The four columns at the side have Roman references and are derived from the design of triumphal arches, with a broad entrance in the centre and two smaller openings at the sides.

The double tympanum is typically baroque: the triangular tympanum, here as in the Cappella Vendramin, has another one over it in the form of an arch. In the synagogue the Tablets of the Law are

inserted between the two geometric shapes, and the whole is topped by the traditional crown, as in the other Scuole. Longhena also used the double tympanum in the entrance to the Giardino Salvi in Vicenza (1645).

The design of this Ark in the Scuola Spagnola was to influence the whole development of the Ark here in Italy and elsewhere in Europe as well; this marble and wood baroque Ark became a kind of prototype. The contrasting colours of the intricate structure are pleasing to the eye, as are the various different materials used: the black marble of the four big striped columns, the white and gold of the Tablets of the Law with the wooden crown above, and the blue of the background.

Detail of the Ark of the Covenant. The Tablets of the Law surmounted by a crown appear between two tympana, in accordance with traditional symbolism.

In theory the use of marble in the interior decoration of synagogues was prohibited, as has been mentioned before; only inexpensive materials like wood and imitation marbling were supposed to be used, and these in fact were virtually the sole materials used in the decoration of the Scuole of the Ghetto Nuovo, apart from a few little touches of real marble. But evidently such regulations were disregarded by the Jews of the Ghetto Vecchio, as both here and in the Scuola Levantina (even more in the latter) polychrome marbles have been used with a certain recklessness. The freedom enjoyed by the two Mediterranean communities to be more ostentatious can be attributed to the higher economic and social status they enjoyed. It is certainly true to say that they were held in greater consideration by the government of the Serenissima and were allowed more privileges, probably because of the contribution they made to commercial life in Venice. The German Jews, who had incorporated the Italian nucleus, had the opposite experience, growing so impoverished as a result of running pawnshops that they were increasingly at the mercy of the magistrature, carefully inspected and heavily taxed.

The shape of the doors of the Ark recalls either the Tablets of the Law or the Gates of Jerusalem; they bear the date 1755 and are usually covered by a heavy curtain of brocade or velvet, sometimes decorated with inscriptions or embroidery. These curtains, called *parokhet*, are an integral part of the design of the Ark. They symbolize the cloth that covered the Holy of Holies in Jerusalem, the Sancta Sanctorum where the Ark and the Tablets of the Law were kept. The cloth is usually decorated with the names of benefactors, and traditional motifs such as vines, twisted columns, eagles, lions and other details from the Temple of Solomon.

The Ark is surrounded by a semicircular wooden balustrade, low and graceful, with double gates decorated with geometric and floral patterns. This dates from the restoration at the end of the nineteenth century, when the *bimah* was used as a choir and the prayer leader's reading-desk was moved to the area right in front of the Ark. At this period the area in front of the Ark was raised by the insertion of a wooden platform. This was not a very satisfactory alteration from a liturgical point of view because it meant that the prayer leader had to turn his back on the congregation (when prayers are said everyone turns towards Jerusalem, which means turning towards the Ark).

Within the balustrade, on the right, a small plaque marks the spot where an unexploded bomb fell. The text reads: 'Here fell a bomb/ it dug itself in/ but did no damage/ it burst in, but with discernment'. Rabbi Abramo Lattes composed a special prayer to mark the event, to be recited every year on the last Friday in August, in memory of the bomb which fell on 17 August 1849. The bomb had been fired by the Austrians at Forte di Marghera during the famous civic uprising against the Austrian occupation in which many Venetian Jews took part.

Daniele Manin, leader of the insurrection, belonged to a family whose origins were Jewish (his grandparents had converted in 1759), and the provisional government of his Independent Republic included Leone Pincherle as Minister of Agriculture and Trade, Isacco Pesar Maurogonato as Minister of Finance, Jacopo Treves de' Bonfil as Minister of Posts, and others as well, including the rabbis Salomone Olper and Abramo Lattes.

Here, as in the other Scuole, the seating is arranged in parallel lines along the side walls leaving a broad aisle in the centre which links the Ark to the *bimah*. The left-hand side is screened off by a wooden grille. The stairs leading to the women's gallery are steep and tiring, so for many years women have been allowed to remain in the main room of the synagogue, symbolically separated from the men by this grille, which is only removed for wedding ceremonies.

Some of the benches on the right, reserved for men, bear small name-plates. The names on the plates are those of living people who carry on the old tradition of reserving their place in the synagogue, although it is no longer strictly necessary. The cost nowadays is just a token, whereas in the past most of the funds available for the maintenance of the synagogue came from the renting of seats.

The elliptical women's gallery is built high up, and lends dignity and unity to the overall impression. If the design of the Ark is openly derived from Christian church architecture, i.e. from the altar, the women's gallery draws on another model, a lay one this time, namely the theatre. It is really no more than a balcony from which (bearing Coryat's description in mind) the lady spectators could participate in the prayers, the readings, the discussions and the singing, just as in the theatre the audience watches the events on the stage from the balconies above.

During the second half of the sixteenth century and the first decades of the seventeenth century, the theatre in Venice really took off. The first permanent theatre, built of stone, was built near San Cassiano in 1565, and by the eighteenth century Venice possessed no fewer than sixteen theatres and was the centre of theatrical life in Europe. The gilded cornice with coronets that decorates the women's gallery in the Scuola Grande Spagnola is typical of seventeenth-century theatre design. The balconies in these theatres were horseshoe-shaped, whereas the one here is elliptical. This shape allows those upstairs to follow what is going on downstairs quite easily; in a synagogue the action is not concentrated in one spot as it is in a theatre, but moves from end to end.

Interior of the Scuola Grande Spagnola, looking towards the Ark of the Covenant. In the style of Longhena, the Ark of the Ponentine Synagogue is reminiscent of the altar designed by him for the Capella Vendramin in S. Pietro di Castello, the former cathedral of Venice.

The ovoidal women's gallery in the Scuola Tedesca was probably inspired by the gallery in the Scuola Grande Spagnola, already the most admired and most influential of the synagogues in Venice. In Vittorio Veneto (formerly Ceneda), in Conegliano and in other northern towns the same treatment of the gallery can be found, with minor variations. The connection between the gallery in the Scuola Spagnola and the gallery in the Scuola Tedesca is reinforced by the similarity of the decoration below the balustrade on both galleries: carved wood with a pattern of alternating rectangles and circles. As noted above, the gallery in the Scuola Tedesca recalls some of the musicians' galleries in eighteenth-century music rooms; these undoubtedly provided a model which would have been more up-to-date than that of the theatres of the preceding century. In any case, the influence of secular architecture, particularly architecture from the sphere of music and the theatre, was very powerful within the walls of the Ghetto, extending even to the synagogues.

In spite of the hostility of the more orthodox rabbis, music was also to become part of the ritual of the synagogue. In 1605 a male choir made its appearance in the Scuola Spagnola, achieving a high standard of musicianship. Leon da Modena, a progressive rabbi who welcomed cultural exchanges with the city of Venice, always defended music in his writings, maintaining that there could be nothing wrong in accompanying the praise of God with music, and that uttering the name of God in hymns could not be considered blasphemous. His views evidently prevailed, since in 1628 he became *maestro di cappella* of the Spagnola synagogue and the head of a musical academy, called in Italian the 'Accademia degli Impediti' (Academy of the Obstructed), in Hebrew 'Bezochrenu et Zion', the name being taken from the last words of the psalm: 'By the waters of Babylon I sat down and wept, as I remembered Zion. On the willows in the middle of the stream we hung up our harps …'

In the same year, 1628, an attempt was made to install an organ in the synagogue, but some of the rabbis drew the line at this. Nevertheless, by the end of the seventeenth century, liturgical music had become the norm in synagogues. The Hebrew singing in the Scuola Spagnola and the Scuola Tedesca did not pass unnoticed. Benedetto Marcello, the great composer, was a familiar figure in the synagogues and composed settings for fifty of the Psalms, ten of them on themes heard in the Scuole of the Ghetto.

The Scuola Spagnola was the only synagogue in Venice eventually to acquire an organ. This happened nearly two hundred and fifty years after the original attempt, and required a fundamental reorganization of the *bimah*. In 1838 Baron Treves de' Bonfil, a prominent member of the community, succeeded, in the face of strong opposition, in founding a women's choir. Nearly sixty years later, in 1893, an organ, donated by some of the members of the community, was installed behind the *bimah*. The architects Fano and Oreffice designed a wooden structure which blocked the front of the *bimah* with a decorative row of imitation organ pipes. This totally altered the original function of the *bimah*. From that day until 1980 the Scuola Spagnola had to manage without its original layout, the *bimah* and the Ark at opposite ends. Only after lengthy negotiations was it agreed recently to dismantle the nineteenth-century decoration and to restore the *bimah* to its former glory as far as possible. The organ remains, half hidden behind a red curtain, which also covers the arch. In fact the organ as an instrument bears no relation to Jewish liturgy; the prayers are intoned by the unaccompanied human voice, being the only instrument permitted. The use of the organ for occasional concerts is tolerated (some Jewish hymns were set to music by the Venetian composer Ermanno Wolf-Ferrari), and for weddings. The old hand-pumped organ is, in fact, seldom used.

In the Scuola Spagnola, the nineteenth-century organ is hidden behind the *bimah*.

The elaborate ceiling with its carved cornices, and the elegant gallery lend an opulent unity to this huge chamber, still the formal venue for gatherings of the Venetian Jewish community.

The *bimah* of the Scuola Grande Spagnola was erected at the end of the nineteenth century, when it housed a women's choir. An organ was added at the time, an element totally alien to Jewish liturgy. In 1980, fake organ pipes replaced the real ones (which concealed the organ) and the *bimah* was restored to its original function.

Nowadays the *bimah* is like an austere raised rectangular pulpit. Two marble columns support an architrave surmounted by an elaborate wooden structure carved with amphoras and scrolls, very different from the calm classicism of the Ark. Like the *bimah* in the Scuola Canton, it resembles a stage, and the drapes enhance this resemblance. David Cassuto, the historian of the Venetian Scuole, points out the resemblance between this, the *bimah* in the Scuola Levantina and the altar by Bernini in Saint Peter's in Rome. The back portion, which is half-hidden by the organ, has a half-cupola decorated in blue and white, badly lit and bearing little chromatic relationship to the rest of the *bimah*. The whole structure seems somehow the least convincing part of the synagogue, possibly because much of the seventeenth-century decoration was lost during the alterations of 1893.

A major contribution to the elegance and harmony of the room is made by the ceiling, richly decorated with mouldings in wood and plaster; this and the women's gallery together, in contrast to the *bimah*, form a beautiful and stylistically coherent whole. This ceiling is reminiscent of the ceiling in Ca'Pesaro, Baldassare Longhena and Antonio Gaspari's imposing palace on the Grand Canal. Both the Palazzo

Pesaro (now a Museum of Modern and Oriental Art) and another building by Longhena, the Palazzo Belloni-Battagia, are quite close to the Ghetto, on the other side of the Grand Canal. This proximity makes more likely the possibility that Longhena had a hand in the design of the Scuola Spagnola, especially as he also worked on the Chiesa degli Scalzi nearby. Longhena also worked for another important foreign community in Venice, the Greek community, whose cultural and religious centre was near Saint Mark's, not far from the Riva degli Schiavoni.

Several large brass candelabras, in the Flemish style, fill the gap between the ceiling and the pews; they are similar to the candelabras in the Scuola Levantina. The ceiling has been restored recently after an unexpected collapse; at the same time the opportunity was taken to replace the leaded lights in the windows with small circles of pale pink glass.

The generous windows, Palladian in their proportions, echo the shape of the Ark and fill the whole room with natural light. On the left-hand side, near the *bimah*, two of the windows are blind, placed there only for the sake of symmetry. This seals the synagogue off from the nearby workshops in the Campiello. The space between the windows is occupied by marbled pilasters decorated with appliqué bands, a device frequently found in other buildings by Longhena. The floor is made of grey and white marble paving stones in concentric squares, which heightens the feeling of cohesion in the room.

In spite of its size the synagogue remains essentially human in scale. Even the Ark, though sumptuously decorated, is of quite modest proportions. The arrangement of the benches on opposite sides reinforces the sense of community, the sense of a meeting-place. There is nothing particularly mystical about this richly decorated baroque room, brilliantly and theatrically lit by a host of candelabras.

A further interesting fact is that the Ponentine Jews, more than any of the communities in the Ghetto Nuovo, were willing to relinquish their own traditions almost completely when they built this synagogue. Compared with the three synagogues in the Ghetto Nuovo, the Scuola Spagnola has almost no wall inscriptions whatsoever, and makes scant reference to the architecture of other synagogues in Italy, or Europe as a whole. It may be that the Marranos, who had left Spain and Portugal some while back, and who had been reconverted to Judaism sometimes only after several generations, had already lost a large part of their liturgical tradition. Perhaps it was because of this lack of cultural hinterland that the Ponentini were more open to outside influences, and were willing to employ the best artists in the city. Longhena, or one of his followers, has managed to fuse together disparate elements into a

The overall view from the top of the gallery reveals the careful symmetry of the whole; in the best Longhenian tradition, exuberant baroque ornament is contained within a classical framework.

unified whole, albeit a highly theatrical one; the adaptation of details borrowed from church, palace and theatre architecture reveals the maturity and wide experience of a consummate artist.

To the left of the *bimah*, cleverly camouflaged by the decoration of the wall, is the entrance to a tiny room, completely lined with wood and with a small window with a grille over it. The peaceful atmosphere of this little study (used today as a store room for prayer books) lingers as you go downstairs; it seems so far removed from the rich and theatrical atmosphere of the synagogue itself. It takes you back to the days of Leon da Modena and Simon Luzzatto, when Venice was one of the most important centres of Judaism in Europe, and rabbis and scholars from all over the world thought of this narrow quarter as an essential stopping-place on their peregrinations, and an essential part of their religious lives.

A small study, reached through a well-camouflaged entrance in the synagogue itself, takes us back to the time, long ago, when Venice was one of the cultural capitals of European Jewry. Each Jewish community had its own collection of prayer books and reference works; each also was governed by an elected committee and kept careful registers of births, deaths and marriages, as well as records of attendance at the School.

A study room on the ground floor of the Scuola Grande Spagnola. In 1893. furniture from the Scuola Coanim, in the Ghetto Nuovo, was removed to this room. For reasons of direction the *aaron* and the *bimah* were placed along the side walls, with the result that they are very close to one another.

On the ground floor the entrance to a little *midrash*, or study and prayer room, is to be found. This room is an elongated rectangle, with rather a low ceiling, entirely lined in walnut and with benches and backrests like the other synagogues. One detail however makes this interior stand apart: the Ark and the *bimah* face one another on one of the long sides, so that they are very close together. The Ark seems to have been altered to fit the room by having its lower half removed; it still seems half squashed by the low ceiling, in spite of this alteration. None of the furniture appears to have been designed for this small room, and it probably all comes from elsewhere in the Ghetto. The room was apparently turned into a *midrash* in 1733 when a large number of students arrived with a group of Ponentine Jews from Livorno. Inscriptions and dates over the door probably refer to this. In 1893, when the synagogue was restored, this room was refurnished with furniture from the Scuola Coanim, originally situated in the Ghetto Nuovo, near the *sotopòrtego* and none of the original decoration has survived.

THE
SCUOLA
LEVANTINA

In the centre of the Campiello delle Scuole in the Ghetto Vecchio is a well made of red marble, simpler than the wells in the Ghetto Nuovo. Around the well a band of white marble decorates the paving stones, but the band is broken on the side nearest the façade of the Scuola Levantina, opposite the Scuola Spagnola, as if the enlargement of the synagogue at some stage had modified the original size of the Campiello.

The façade of the Scuola Levantina bears a striking resemblance to the Collegio Greco Flangini, built by Longhena in 1678 with a bequest from Tommaso Flangini. The resemblance goes right down to details: the small oval windows below the cornice, the patterns between the large arched windows with their decorative bars, the rusticated dado (also to be found in another building by Longhena, the Scuola Grande dei Carmini), the window sills and the cornices.

On 2 June 1541 the Senate agreed that the Levantine Jewish merchants could take up residence in the Ghetto Vecchio, consisting at the time of a few houses, large parks and gardens. They thus honoured the request of a small but influential group of people who had hitherto been living, as has been shown (although the official documents make no mention of the fact), inside the Ghetto Nuovo. The agreement of 1541 marks the official recognition of the 'oriental' group in the Ghetto, and must have heralded a substantial improvement in their living conditions, the Ghetto Vecchio being indubitably less chaotic and overcrowded than the Ghetto Nuovo, which had been inhabited by the 'Todeschi' for twenty-five years already.

According to a widely accepted oral tradition, the first Levantine synagogue was built in 1538, three years before the official admission of the Levantini into the Ghetto Vecchio. This date is accepted by many scholars, including both Roth and Pinkerfeld, although it is not based on any written evidence. It is certain, however, that the synagogue was exactly where it is today: a document dated 1610 locates it 'at the back of the Campiello del Pozzo'. It is known that the layout of the previous Scuola was very similar to the one that has come down to us: a huge hall on the ground floor, some smaller rooms for the study of religious texts, a double staircase up to the *piano nobile*, and a main room with a women's gallery over the entrance.

This is the only Scuola to have been purpose-built as a synagogue, and not adapted from another existing building, as the other four had been, which resulted in their inclusion of private apartments and other rooms. A document dating from April 1680 informs us that at that time the Consiglio della Nazione Levantina (Council of the Levantine Community) was considering the total demolition of the existing synagogue and the proposal to build another, larger one. The decision to

Interior of the Scuola Levantina, looking towards the *bimah*. The place where the officiating elder stands, high above the congregation, is illuminated by bright, natural light coming in through the semi-hexagonal *liagò*.

Few of the traditional occupations of the area remain today. There is a furniture restorer, a junk shop pretending to be an antique shop, an inn and a baker, the latter selling Jewish Easter sweets all the year round.

Campiello delle Scuole in the Ghetto Vecchio. The unusually ornate façade of the Scuola Levantina is in stark contrast to the buildings around it. Its plan repeats many of the stylistic tricks used in the Collegio Flangini, near the Venetian church of S. Giorgio dei Greci, by Longhena.

Offertory box in Istrian stone, in the entrance to the Scuola Levantina.

adopt this proposal may have been due to the increase in the numbers of the community, or equally to the desire to compete, in size and grandeur, with the nearby Scuola Spagnola, built sometime in the middle of the seventeenth century in the style of Baldassare Longhena.

It is certainly true to say that the façade of the Scuola Levantina is much grander and more harmonious than that of the Scuola Spagnola, which has some awkward corners. In fact the Levantine synagogue is the only 'beautiful' building in the Ghetto; seen from the Fondamenta di Cannaregio it is an imposing sight, in stark contrast to the buildings that surround it.

Curiously enough, the doorway on the main façade is not the principal entrance to the synagogue, which is on the side. On the Campiello side there are two inscriptions worthy of note: one, in the centre, records the destruction of the Temple in Jerusalem, and the other, near the corner between the two rows of windows, commemorates the Venetian Jews who fell in the First World War.

The two large arched doorways are equal in size and both are protected above by a projecting corbel; this design is repeated over the windows of the first floor. The heavy wooden doors are contemporary with the construction of the synagogue and are richly carved with floral designs, characterized by Elena Bassi as 'sensuous' in their baroque opulence. The composition of the designs is freer than that of the doors of the Scuola Spagnola, where the carving is contained within a geometrical framework. From the side, where the main entrance is to be

found, the synagogue presents many of the same stylistic characteristics that were found on the front. One detail catches the eye, however, up on the first floor where the main hall of the synagogue is situated – an elegant closed balcony, polygonal in shape, covered by a small, eaved roof which has a sort of little up-turned pyramid on top. The correct Venetian term for this is a '*liagò*', and the *liagò* is a familiar sight in Venice. Originating in the East, it underwent various modifications over the centuries, adapting itself to changing fashions in architecture. The *liagò* is often to be found on the side walls of palazzi, projecting from the wall, particularly along the narrowest canals and the darkest alleyways. It helps to bring more light to the interior, and of course also gives vitality and interest to the exterior. It was particularly popular during the baroque period because of the theatrical possibilities it offered, and is quite commonly found in palaces attributed to Longhena or to one of his followers. The *liagò* on the Scuola Levantina bears a striking resemblance to the one on the lateral façade of the Ca'Rezzonico, designed by Longhena himself and to the one on the Scuola dei Luganegheri on the Zattere.

It must be stressed here that this detail from palace architecture, grafted artlessly on to the side of a synagogue, fits perfectly. Similar graftings have already been noted in the Scuola Canton and the Scuola Italiana, though this building is much more sophisticated and prominent than its 'sisters' in the Ghetto Nuovo.

Once the Scuola Luzzatto (which moved from the Ghetto Nuovo) was rebuilt into the ground floor of the Scuola Levantina in 1836, the main entrance to the Levantine synagogue ceased to be used because it led straight into the other Scuola; this explains why the side door is used today. The side door is asymmetrically placed with respect to the *liagò*, and this irregularity has led people to assume that the second door was only constucted in the nineteenth century, to make the Scuola Luzzatto more spacious. It seemed reasonable to conclude that the entrance on the Campiello was originally the only entrance because it connects accurately with the double staircase leading up to the synagogue. Documentary evidence, however, proves that this is not the case: there were always two doors, exactly in the position they are in today, and we can only guess at the reason for the awkward placing of the second one.

Whatever the reason, the result is that the interior of the Scuola Levantina is reached at an unnatural angle. The hall is rectangular, and a garden can be seen through the window at the back. A richly carved band of walnut runs the length of the four walls at cornice height, below the exposed beams of the ceiling. The hall is similar in feeling to the hall of the nearby Scuola Ponentina, but the decoration is finer here; note for instance the exceptional candelabras. To the left of the entrance an original stone handbasin is still in use. On the left wall a plaque commemorates the visit of Sir Moses Montefiore, the English philanthropist, famous for the support he gave to Jewish communities throughout the world; here, at the venerable age of 93, he 'raised his voice to God in prayer'. In the Ghetto Vecchio there is still a huge hall used for meetings which is dedicated to this generous benefactor, who lived to the age of 101.

There are offertory boxes on both sides of the hall, one of which is particularly fine. Made of carved white stone, it bears the inscription: 'Box for the labours of the Signori Levantini' and is in the shape of the 'bocche della verità', the 'mouths of truth', holes in the wall to be found in the Palazzo Ducale which were designed to receive secret denunciations. On the right, in front of the small door that leads to the stairs, is the entrance to the Scuola Luzzatto.

SCUOLA LUZZATTO

As has already been noted, the Scuola Luzzatto was originally on the Campo del Ghetto Nuovo, on the side of the Campo that was demolished in the nineteenth century, where the Casa di Riposo is today.

Interior of the Scuola Luzzatto, looking towards the Ark. In spite of its being moved and rebuilt, it retains an intense feel of the sixteenth century. Recent restoration has returned it to its former glory.

Interior of the Scuola Luzzatto, looking towards the *bimah*. Dating from the late sixteenth century, this room dedicated to prayer and study was originally in the Ghetto Nuovo. In 1836 it was moved and rebuilt on the ground floor of the Scuola Levantina.

The Scuola Luzzatto was moved to this building and rebuilt inside the ground floor of the Scuola Levantina in 1836. The furniture had to be modified to suit the new surroundings – a long rectangular room with the Ark and the *bimah* on the two shorter walls. Because this is not a real synagogue but a *yeshiva*, a study room for advanced religious studies, there is no women's gallery. Apart from that it is furnished just like a synagogue.

The Ark is particularly fine, and may be the oldest *aaron* to be found in the Venetian Ghetto. It is of Renaissance design, made entirely of wood with gilding on a green background. The elegant patterns on the doors recall the Lombardic decorations in the church of S. Maria dei Miracoli. The wooden railing around the *aaron* was added in the nineteenth century and is modelled on the railings in the Scuola Italiana and the Scuola Spagnola. As usual, the benches are arranged along the longer walls, visually and spiritually uniting the Ark and the *bimah*. The door that leads on to the Campiello (never used today) interrupts the side opposite the entrance, destroys the harmony of the whole and betrays the fact that this was not the original seat of the Scuola Luzzatto. The *bimah* is raised on four steps and is simple in design. Above it is a nineteenth-century canopy.

The walls are panelled with wood, and poetic inscriptions extolling God decorate the panels. The combined initials of the inscriptions form the name Elihau Aròn Hazach. It is not impossible that the idea of an acrostic inscription (whose initial letters form a word, in this case a name) may have been the inspiration for similar panels in the Scuola Italiana. The ceiling, with its very dense exposed beams, is of Renaissance design. Although the Scuola was moved from one place to another, its anonymous architects succeeded in preserving its atmosphere. This is the only interior in the Ghetto which still has a sixteenth-century air, introverted and calm, and unsullied by the rich, sometimes excessive decoration of the baroque and rococo periods. David Cassuto, in his study of the synagogues of Venice, draws an interesting parallel between the Scuola Luzzatto, roughly dating from the end of the sixteenth century, and the Scuola Dalmata di San Giorgio (also known as the Scuola degli Schiavoni), whose ground-floor room was remodelled in 1551. He notes certain similarities in the interiors, between the Ark and the altar, for example, and between the bands running right round the walls at ceiling level, wooden here in the *yeshiva* and marble in San Giorgio.

Beyond these surface similarities, which are quite plausible as the artists used in both places were local, the Scuola Luzzatto is simple and unspoiled, very different from the other two synagogues in the Ghetto

Vecchio. This one transports us away from pomp and show to the world of prayer and study, far removed from the thoughts about maritime trade which must have occupied the waking hours of the Sephardic merchants; it gives an idea of what the Scuole of the Ghetto Nuovo must have been like before they were filled with the finery and gilding of the eighteenth century.

After one restoration in 1950, the Scuola Luzzatto was again remodelled between 1974 and 1981, thanks to a grant from the 'Save Venice' fund in New York and the personal assistance of Mrs Danielle Garner Luzzatto, a descendant of the original family. All the wall panelling, which was beginning to split at the bottom, was removed. The framework was reinforced with wedges of larch wood; wooden supports for the panelling were fixed to the wall with cement. Certain areas of the interior were completely rebuilt. All the wood was chemically treated against rot and was then given two coats of wax. The original flooring, lozenge-shaped tiles in contrasting colours, was too far gone to be restored and was replaced with terra-cotta tiles from Florence. The limewood Ark was cleaned and restored, the removal of thick layers of dark varnish by chemical cleaners revealing the original painting. The Dutch-style lamps are new, and similar to the ones already in the building.

The Scuola Luzzatto is no longer a study and common room for learned and religious men; it is virtually unused nowadays. It was however opened up recently on the occasion of the marriage of one of the Luzzatto family.

In front of the entrance to the *yeshiva* a small door gives access to the double staircase that leads to the big Levantine synagogue on the first floor. On the left, near the door, a small metal plaque records the termination of the restoration financed by the 'Save Venice' fund in 1975.

Between the two flights of stairs, on the wall, an eighteenth-century plaque, similar to those found in the synagogues in the Ghetto Nuovo, reads: 'Humble in deed and of loyal faith, each devout person comes here to offer up his prayers, and as he turns away to leave, thoughts of God continue to fill his mind'. The Hebrew version makes an acrostic in which the name of God is formed by the initial letters of the first word in every line.

The two entrances to the Scuola Levantina both enter through one of the long sides, differing in this from the Scuola Spagnola. Here the entrances are on the gallery side, one door being near the Ark and the other almost hidden by the huge *bimah*.

Interior of the Scuola Levantina, looking towards the *bimah*, during the festival of Purim. The synagogue is in regular use today during the months of October to April.

Scuola Levantina: detail of the *bimah*. Oral tradition attributes this and the ceiling to the famous craftsman in wood, Andrea Brustolon (1662–1732), from Belluno; Brustolon carved highly ornate, baroque wooden furniture.

The Scuola Levantina is the richest in decoration, and the most dramatically coloured, of all the synagogues in Venice. The black carved wood, the fiery red of the curtains, the sparkle of the innumerable lamps completely fill the space, giving no rest to the eye, no opportunity to pause gratefully on a smooth, empty surface. The artist, or artists, obviously wanted to compensate for the lack of pictures with a vast profusion of ornament unrivalled in any of the other synagogues in the Ghetto.

It is undoubtedly the *bimah*, on the right, that catches the eye first, that is once the eyes have become accustomed to the excessive opulence of the decoration in this very unusual interior. The large wooden pulpit is the most elaborate item in the whole Ghetto, and either its superabundant originality attracts, or its exaggerated ornamentation repels. It is evident at once that the *bimah* is disproportionately large for a room this size (43 x 28 feet/13.3 x 8.5 metres). A double staircase leads to the high platform where the prayer leader sits; he is closer to the women's gallery than he is to the room below. At the foot of the staircases are two carved wooden fruit bowls, brimming with oversized baroque fruit. Under the parapet, between the two staircases, is a beautifully carved cupboard door. The carving is so fine that this might well be the door of an Ark; it is, in fact, the door to the cupboard where the books are kept. Every synagogue has always had a *ghenizà*, a cupboard or storeroom where prayer books or religious books which are no longer in use are kept. Out of respect, they are never thrown out nor are loose pages thrown away.

The prayer leader's platform is brightly lit from above, the light coming from the semi-hexagonal lantern on the top of the *liagò* already described on the side wall of the synagogue. The effect of the natural light is to mitigate the overpowering, riotous architecture and to give it an almost diaphanous quality. Two large, highly theatrical spiral columns rise from the parapet (which is also completely covered in carving) and reach right up to the ceiling, where they gradually disappear in a series of cornices, declining in size as they get closer to the top.

Tradition has it, though, as so often, no documentary evidence exists, that this remarkable structure was designed by the artist Andrea Brustolon from Belluno (1662–1732). He was well known in Venice for the collection of furniture he made between 1700 and 1723 for the Venier family from San Vio, forty pieces in all. (The Venier furniture is now in Ca'Rezzonico, the museum of eighteenth-century Venice; the chairs are in the Quirinale in Rome.) He also made twelve large chairs representing the months for the Pisana family villa at Strà. Brustolon was the greatest of the cabinet makers of the Veneto during the late

Scuola Levantina: detail of the *bimah*. Two vast twisted columns, surmounted by pompous capitals in pure bronze, were posted at the entrance to the Temple of Solomon. This tradition (followed also by Bernini) inspired the person who created the *bimah* in the Scuola Levantina.

Interior of the Scuola Levantina, showing the *bimah*.

seventeenth and early eighteenth centuries, and was admired for his imagination and vision, and for the extraordinary elegance of his furniture.

The spiral columns are connected with one of the most important features of the Temple of Solomon: it is believed that two enormous columns were placed at the entrance to the temple, with heavy cast bronze capitals, and the trunks of two palm trees growing nearby were intertwined with the columns. The two mysterious columns, probably of Phoenician handiwork, were to become for centuries a powerful religious symbol in both Jewish and Christian art. It was not chance that led Bernini to use the symbol when he rebuilt the most important Christian church in the world, the heart of the Catholic faith, Saint Peter's in Rome. The author of this baldaquin, Brustolon, or a lesser artist in the same circle, had certainly been to Rome. In fact the spiral columns must have been quite familiar to artists working in Venice, even before the arrival of Bernini. The motif is used very frequently in the architectural backgrounds of painters like Paolo Veronese, in scenes often inspired by the Old Testament (for example the story of Esther and Ahasuerus on the ceiling of S. Sebastiano). The sinuous columns of the baldaquin in the synagogue are not as sedate as the columns in Veronese's paintings; the shapes entwine with a sort of animal energy, reminiscent of the sea-serpents and monsters invented by Brustolon on the armchairs for the Venier family. The same design can be found in Venice, in the late sixteenth-century church of the Scalzi, and also in a later church, the Gesuiti on the Fondamente Nuove. The graceful spiral columns in the Scuola Canton have none of the baroque exuberance of their cousins in the Scuola Levantina; they display a lightness and elegance which presages the Art Nouveau.

The frequent recurrence of decoration based on fruit – on the columns, on the central swag which culminates in a bunch of grapes, on the stair parapet – is also perfectly consistent with Jewish tradition, being particularly connected with the celebration of certain feast days when the fruits of the earth are praised. Sukkot is one of these; it is connected with ancient harvest festivals, when branches of cedar and palm would be brought to the synagogue.

The top of the canopy merges into the ceiling, the latter probably decorated by the artist who designed the *bimah*. Perhaps if the ceiling had been higher the artist would have devised a more elaborate canopy, with scroll work on top as in the Scuola Spagnola, where the decoration of the baldaquin is based on the high altar in Saint Peter's. The solution forced on the artist by lack of space is a very elegant one anyway: the canopy is fixed directly to the ceiling.

The climax of the magnificently decorated ceiling is the central caisson, formed by concentric ornamental cornices in a typically Venetian design. This design here is different, however; whereas in other Venetian palaces the cornices outline the space reserved for paintings, here the cornices are the main ornamental feature, reversing the usual effect. The wooden cornices stand out against the pale-coloured plaster, and the result is very striking. Both the *bimah* and the ceiling are in dark stained walnut, contrasting very starkly with the white background. The black-white contrast, ebony and ivory, enhanced by recent cleaning has been the subject of widespread criticism because it is thought not to reflect the original colour scheme.

The overall effect is very exciting, largely because the *bimah* and the ceiling, with their opulent ornamentation, go together so perfectly, enriching and enlivening the whole interior. If the room had been a little larger the effect might have been a little less overpowering. The *bimah* gives the impression that at any moment it will break out of the narrow space allotted to it. Much more sober in design (and not really to be compared) are the benches, also in walnut; a simple carved rosette decorates the central panel. They may be slightly older than the other wooden items. Small name tags mark the reserved seats in the synagogue.

Conspicuous here are seven beautiful brass candelabras, six smaller ones with a larger one in the middle. Tradition has it that they were given to the Levantines by the famous Portuguese synagogue in Amsterdam (still functioning today). What is not in dispute is the existence of very close ties, both commercial and intellectual, between the Jewish communities in Venice, and the communities in the 'Venice of the North'. For a long period the two cities competed for the position of capital of European Jewry.

The bare simplicity of the women's gallery is in strong contrast to the elegance of the main chamber. The gallery runs right across the entrance wall.

The women's gallery on the long wall above the two doors into the synagogue is architecturally unremarkable. Perhaps lack of space again imposed a modest design, reminiscent of the simple galleries in the Scuola Italiana and the Scuola Canton, rather than a grandiose affair like the balcony in the Scuola Spagnola. In the Scuola Spagnola the women's gallery is very difficult of access and has fallen into disuse but here the women still go up to their balcony, and the grilles, which are still visible, have not been closed for many years. The Scuola Levantina is in regular use today. It is normally used between the religious festivals of the autumn (the last of which is Simhat Torah, the Festival of the Torah) and the following spring, when Pesach is over. The weekly celebrations on Friday evening and Saturday take place here, and the winter festivals of Hanukah and Purim. The synagogue seen from the gallery is a spectacular sight, particularly when the lamps light up the dark wood and the red curtains and drapes. The precious damask cloth in the panels below the women's gallery might be connected with the 'Levantine' origins of this community, and with the traditions they imported from Spain and from the Orient; such damasks are to be found in Venetian churches as well. They were used to cover the columns during solemn seasons like Lent. The Tránsito synagogue, in Toledo, was covered all over inside, to a height of nearly seventeen feet (five metres), with precious fabrics. Unfortunately the red damask in the Scuola Levantina is in bad repair; holes were made in it to allow the insertion of hot air central-heating pipes!

The Levantine synagogue, like the Ponentine, has few wall inscriptions. The Sephardic community had little concern for tradition, and allowed the Venetian artists in their employ to use their own imaginations, probably giving them scant guidance. There are one or two inscriptions over the door, both dating from the eighteenth century. Above the door near the Ark the inscription reads: 'In Thee, Oh Lord, have I placed my hope', and above the arch: 'When this place is worthy of reverence, then is it none other than the House of God' (Jacob's dream, *Genesis*). Above the other door, near the *bimah*, is the date 1786; above the arch two verses from the *Psalms*: 'Open unto me the gates of Justice, that I may bring there the praise of the Lord', and 'This is the door of the Lord, the Just may enter here'.

Above the women's gallery is a decoration made of coloured glass, with squares repeating two symbols, both referring to Solomon and both frequently used on the plaques in the Cemetery of San Nicolo: the knot, and the five-pointed star. These details bear no relation to anything else in the synagogue, and were installed in the first years of this century.

Jewish orthodoxy still dictates that women should sit separately in the upstairs gallery provided for them. Until a few decades ago the wooden grilles, which can still be seen, remained lowered.

The Ark should not be overlooked, although it is inevitably overshadowed by the presence of the extraordinary *bimah* described above. In fact this Ark strongly resembles the one in the Scuola Spagnola, but it is if anything more opulently decorated with costly marbles. It achieves its effect by the combination of different coloured marbles, after the oriental fashion which was always popular in Venice, from the polychrome marbles in Saint Mark's onwards.

The classical architrave, decorated with amphora and pine-tree designs, is supported by four columns of striped grey marble, mounted on high plinths and surmounted by Corinthian capitals. There is a second architrave above the first one, just as in the Scuola Spagnola, then an arch with a blue background, smaller however than its twin in the Scuola Spagnola. The writing on the second architrave, in gold on a black background, reads as follows: 'I shall bow down my head in the temple of Thy Holiness, and shall magnify Thy Name' (from the *Psalms*). The little gold plaque over the inscription quotes the precept from the Talmud: 'Know ye before Whom you stand'. On the door of the Ark is the date '1782'. The base of the Ark bears a series of geometrical carvings in grey and red marble. The whole structure is four steps higher than the rest of the room, and is encircled by a balustrade in red Verona marble, with small columns in polychrome marble. The low brass gate is neoclassical and was 'the gift of the beloved Rabbi Menachem, son of Maimon Vivante, to the Lord in the year (I thank Thee from the bottom of my heart) 5546–1786'. Inside the balustrade are some massive brass candlesticks, matched above by a series of silver lamps hanging from the ceiling. In front of the *ner tamid* (the eternal flame) stands a large silver lamp, a seventeenth-century piece which was formerly in the Scuola Italiana; because of its heavy shape, it is known as '*el pignaton*', the big pot.

The Ark has no particularly original features, and is remarkable largely because of the opulence of the materials used. The uninhibited use of materials such as marble in direct contravention of the Venetian government's prohibitions, suggests that the Levantine community, even more than the Ponentine, enjoyed greater privileges than the other Jews of the Ghetto; one privilege was the uninhibited display of their worldly wealth.

The Ark of the Covenant in the Scuola Levantina is similar to the Ark in the nearby Grande Scuola Spagnola, but even more ornate. Here the oriental taste for contrasting bands of marble (as in the Basilica di S. Marco) is indulged.

Detail of the entrance to the Ghetto Vecchio on the Fondamenta di Cannaregio. On the door jambs of Istrian stone on either side of the *sotopòrtego*, two holes can be seen where the wooden gates that used to be closed from sundown to sunrise were fixed. The gates were finally discarded by municipal decree by the provisory government on 7 July 1797.

Ghetto Vecchio: slab commemorating 20 September 1704. Just before you reach the *sotopòrtego* that leads to the Fondamenta di Cannaregio, a slab bears the list of punishments to be meted out to those who, having converted to Christianity, maintain any contact whatsoever with the Ghetto.

After the Campiello, the Ghetto becomes a little narrower and less prosperous than the part that has already been described. The few shops that remain still reflect the traditional trades of the Ghetto: an antique furniture restorer, a junk shop pretending to be an antique shop, a tavern and a baker who sells Jewish Easter cakes: *zuccherini*, *bisse* and *impàde*.

On the right-hand side of this street, just before the *sotopòrtego*, an almost illegible plaque casts a dramatic light on the way of life of the inhabitants of the quarter and testifies to the severity of the Venetian government, in spite of its reputation for tolerance and moderation. The inscription, dated 20 September 1704, warns: 'His Serene Highness and My Lords the Executors against blasphemy forbid any Jew or Jewess who has been converted to Christianity to enter the Ghetto of this city under any pretext whatsoever'. In cases of disobedience, the guilty person would be punished with 'rope, prison, the galley, the lash, the pillory'; informers would be rewarded with a percentage of the goods confiscated from the luckless converts.

The severity of this injunction gives some idea of the attempt by the magistrature to curb a phenomenon which was certainly very prevalent, a type of Marranism which must have been very difficult to wipe out. It is obvious that many Jews would see baptism as a way out of the Ghetto, but that they would remain tied to their former life in many respects. The repeatedly imposed obligation on Jews to wear a cap of a certain colour in order to be instantly recognizable also bears witness to the government's desire to prevent any kind of mixing between Jews and Christians, particularly between the sexes. The menacing tone of these threats is not easily ignored.

The *sotopòrtego* brings us out of the Ghetto to the busy, airy Fondamenta di Cannaregio by the canal. Looking back at the Ghetto, the walled-up windows of the guardhouse are visible in the wall and the door-jamb still bears the holes where the bolts of the gate were drawn at night. The Ghetto leaves an impression of violent contrasts: luxury and poverty, freedom and segregation – a microcosm in fact of the condition of mankind. It is difficult not to dwell on the themes of injustice, intolerance and the uncertainty of life.

THE GHETTO NUOVISSIMO

Palazzo Treves in the Ghetto Nuovissimo. Occupying a prime position on the Rio d S. Girolamo, Palazzo Treves, in the style of Sansovino, is the most conspicuous building in the Ghetto.

Doorway to the Ghetto Nuovissimo – more spacious and elegant than the entrances to the other Ghettos. The Ghetto Nuovissimo was largely residential and contained no shops or synagogues. The entrance is more imposing than any of the others.

The Ghetto Nuovissimo offers fresh proof of the unequal treatment meted out to the various communities within the Ghetto; it was created in March 1633 to house the more privileged newcomers to the Ghetto, when the Levantine and Ponentine Jews requested and obtained a new, more comfortable residential area from the magistrature of the Cinque Savi alla Mercanzia; this would allow new families of Sephardic merchants to come and live in Venice. The Ghetto Nuovo and the Ghetto Vecchio were not overcrowded at the time, the plague of 1630–31 having claimed a large number of victims; more than twenty dwellings were vacant in the Jewish quarter. In spite of this the Government, aware of a grave economic crisis in the State of Venice, thought it opportune to grant the request, hoping thereby to inject new energy into commercial life. A new residential area was quickly found, near the Ghetto Nuovo, in the Contrada di San Marcuola, with space enough to accommodate at least twenty families in comfort.

The new sector is much smaller than the other two and is really an extension of the Campo del Ghetto Nuovo. It is situated at the confluence of the Rio de S. Girolamo and the Rio del Ghetto Nuovo (then the Rio della Macina), and is reached through the same *sotopòrtego* that leads to the Ghetto Nuovo, turning left after the bridge. The ground plan of the Ghetto Nuovissimo is very simple: two intersecting streets join three big blocks of houses, two of which face the canal. The streets have doorways at either end, gated in previous centuries; the doorway on the Calle degli Ormesini is quite distinctive, being decorated with a pattern of smooth bosses.

The Ghetto Nuovissimo differed from the other two sectors of the Ghetto in not possessing the variety of little businesses which drew all sorts of different people to the area during the day, nor was there any of the life that took place around the synagogues; this Ghetto had neither shops nor synagogues (a school is the only institution known to have existed there) so it was in practice simply a residential quarter for the wealthier Jews. Today the area is rather shabby, and the silent streets give a feeling of abandonment rather than privilege.

The most decent-looking building today is the large house occupying the prime position on the Rio di S. Girolamo. It is a twin palace, with two elegant entrance porches (note the sculptured heads in the keystones), vaguely reminiscent of Sansovino. In the eighteenth century this was the residence of the dei Treves, one of the richest banking families in the history of the Venetian Ghetto.

The best side of this building, architecturally, is the side along the canal that is visible from the Ghetto Nuovo. It is extremely stately, particularly in contrast to the other buildings in the Ghetto; it would not

look out of place on the Grand Canal. In fact the Treves family eventually went to live on the Grand Canal, once segregation was no longer in force. There are two double doors giving straight on to the canal to connect the palace directly with the outside world.

The building along the Rio di Ghetto Nuovo belonged to the Vivante family in the eighteenth century; although of interest architecturally, it is in such a state of disrepair nowadays that it looks more like a shabby suburban block of flats than a dignified small palace. The endless lines of washing stretched between the Ghetto Nuovissimo and the Ghetto Nuovo add a touch of colour to the dilapidated walls.

To complete this tour of the Ghetto, and to delve further into the history of the Jews in Venice, it is time now to take a vaporetto to the Lido, and there to walk northwards along the lagoon to the old cemetery of S. Nicolo.

The Treves, one of the richest banking families in the whole history of the Ghetto, lived there during the second half of the eighteenth century. Worthy of note are the twin doors at canal level, giving direct contact with the outside world.

Palazzo Treves and Palazzo Vivante, Ghetto Nuovissimo. The Ghetto Nuovissimo is the smallest of the three sections of the Ghetto and was established in 1633 to house twenty or so Sephardic families.

THE CEMETERY OF S. NICOLO DEL LIDO

The oldest part of the cemetery can be visited on application to the custodian of the nearby Cimitero Nuovo, still used today by the Jewish Community of Venice.

The oldest tombstone in the cemetery dates back to 1389. In artistic terms, the most interesting graves are those of the seventeenth and eighteenth centuries. In the eighteenth century the wealthier families adopted the use of the sarcophagus.

A visit to the two Jewish cemeteries, the old and the new, on the Lido, is a must for anyone who has come to Venice in search of the past. Here, following in the footsteps of Goethe and Byron, the visitor can enjoy the silence of one of the emptiest corners of the island. The sun filters through the thicket of ivy and elder, dappling the white tombstones of Istrian stone, lighting up the bas reliefs on the Roman sarcophagi. Symbols, inscriptions, the cracks in the stone no longer instil fear with their intimations of mortality; the site is so peaceful, enveloped in the soft light of the lagoon, that it soothes the spirit, transporting it to a dimension beyond the reach of time and history.

Around the middle of the fourteenth century groups of Jews were beginning to come down to Venice from Northern Europe and the German-speaking countries, to escape from persecution following the terrible outbreak of Black Death in 1348. Other groups were arriving from the southern and central provinces of Italy in search of better living conditions, and a less oppressive legislation than that of the Papal government.

Jewish moneylenders congregated particularly in Treviso and Mestre, but in 1382, after lengthy negotiations, they were given the right to move to Venice with the rest.

This took place immediately after the War of Chioggia, waged between 1378 and 1381 against the Genoese, which had emptied the coffers of the Serenissima. It was hoped that the arrival of new capital from abroad would very soon alleviate the situation. In 1385 the

The old Jewish cemetery of S. Nicolo del Lido, one of the most interesting in Europe, was the object of many pilgrimages in the last century. Visitors were fascinated by the solitude and decay they found there.

contract allowing certain Jewish families from Mestre to set up as moneylenders in the city was renewed for another ten years; they would work through the pawnshops. In 1386 the Signoria received a request from these Jews for a site within the city where they could have their own graveyard. No documents have survived to explain the choice of the site near S. Nicolo del Lido. It was probably simply that the area was sparsely populated, and also a reasonable distance from the city centre. The only important building nearby was the Benedictine convent of S. Nicolo di Mira (founded in 1043), strategically placed at the mouth of the Porto del Lido, and surrounded by vineyards and vegetable gardens which stretched right down to the seashore.

One of these vineyards was made over by the magistrature of Piòvego to Salamone di Santa Sofia and Crisanto di Sant'Aponal, representatives of the Jewish community of Venice. The land in question was defined as agricultural land with no buildings on it. The owner of the land is not named, nor is any payment for use of the land mentioned. We know that the land covered a rectangular site, seventy by thirty feet, between the sea and the lagoon and on the Venice side of the island.

The symbols carved on the gravestones are sometimes emblems of cities or states, or sometimes they are biblical references. Hands raised in benediction, the harp, the tree of life, the crown of the Torah. Also common are references to the Cabala and to astrology.

The Benedictines in the nearby monastery laid claim to the site and brought the matter to the courts. The case between the monks and the Piòvego (a kind of state property office) lasted a good three years. Agreement was reached in February, 1389, when the monks finally granted possession to the Jews, specifying that the land must be used only as a cemetery. Meanwhile a dwelling for the guardian of the land had been built, featured on old maps of the Lido as 'Casa di Zudei'. In fact there was never a formal conveyancing of the land from the convent to the Jews, because of the prohibition against the ownership of property.

Thenceforth relations between the monks and the Jews were without incident. Numerous requests for more land were made as the community grew. There was an emergency in 1630–1631 when plague decimated the Ghetto community. A plaque marking a common grave records this dramatic event: it bears the inscription 'Jews, 1631'. The situation was regularized in the meantime, and the cemetery was leased to the Jews in perpetuity; an annual rent was fixed, to be paid on the Feast of Saint Michael, in September.

A simple stone marks the common grave of all those who died during the terrible plague of 1630–31.

Between 1671 and 1675 there was an interruption when the area nearest the port had to be fortified because of the war between the Venetians and the Turks. After this everything returned to normal. Strategic and defensive requirements, and gradual erosion of the coastline, led to the slow decline of the cemetery from the late eighteenth century onwards. During the French occupation (1797–8) some headstones and graves which were getting in the way of fortification work were removed, and the surrounding wall was demolished. At the end of the century, burials were suspended and in the nineteenth century a new area was designated, farther from the lagoon, which more or less corresponds with the present Cimitero Nuovo in the Via Cipro. The present Art Nouveau entrance was designed by the architect Guido Costante Sullam (1924).

The atmosphere of desolation and decay attracted poets and writers visiting Venice and they would frequently make the trip to the Lido, a lonely and wild island at that time. Byron and Shelley went riding there in 1818, George Sand and Alfred de Musset had one of their famous quarrels there (de Musset described his companion, in a furious temper, as 'leaping from tomb to tomb'). In the middle of the century Théophile Gautier tells how he found the cemetery in a state of complete abandonment, the gravestones all uprooted and scattered about, and a crowd of children playing amongst them.

Wild plants and sand, together with land subsidence and erosion by the sea, gradually engulfed the graves. In 1884, when the Lido was being built up as a seaside resort, part of the land was taken over for target practice. Excavations have revealed plaques from many different periods, confirming theories about the size of the cemetery: it was large, extending almost from the side of the monastery as far as the shooting-range. The plaques and other remains were placed at the entrance of a smaller enclosure, where the graves of members of the Spanish community used to be.

Between 1925 and 1929 further roadworks by the Cimitero Nuovo uncovered more tombstones, which were re-erected in the Cimitero Nuovo itself. During these roadworks in 1929 the tombs of two outstanding personages were discovered: Leon da Modena and Elia Levita. The discovery was also made of the tombstone of Sara Copio Sullam, the poetess, whose epitaph is said to have been written by Leon da Modena himself, as she was his friend and disciple. Also buried here were Simone Luzzatto, rabbi and man of culture, Leon da Modena's collaborator and successor, and Daniel Rodriga, leader of the Ponentine community and developer of the port of Spalato.

The inscriptions on the tombstones are in Hebrew. Some bear a name and the date of the person's death in Spanish or Portuguese.

Besides uncovering the graves of important people, and revealing the artistry of many tombstones and sarcophagi, these excavations have also made an important contribution to the study of Italian Jewish names and the coats of arms of the most important families. It was mainly the Spanish and Portuguese hidalgos who continued to use their family crests when in exile: the Abendenas, Carbalhos, Fonsecas, Jesurums, Valenzins and Sassos.

Other carved symbols that have come to light are emblems of cities and states, or biblical motifs: the hands raised in blessing (coat of arms of the Cohen family), King David's harp, the tree of life, the crown of the Torah, or references to the Cabala and astrology – stars, the sun and other planets.

From the eighteenth century onwards, richly carved vaults, often decorated all over with leaves and fruit, replaced burial in the ground. The oldest plaque dates from 1389 and commemorates Samuel, son of Samson.

Funeral ceremonies were supervised by the Brotherhood of Mercy. Each nationality had its own area of the cemetery, just as in the Ghetto they had their own Scuole. After the establishment of the Ghetto in 1516, Jewish funerals would go by gondola down the Rio di Cannaregio, along the northern boundary of the city, and then would set out across the lagoon for the northern tip of the Lido. It seems that in the second half of the seventeenth century funerals avoided passing under the bridge of S. Pietro di Castello, then the seat of the Patriarch, in order to avoid hostility, sometimes expressed in the throwing of rubbish and filth. The mortuary of the present Jewish community in Venice is still in the Campo di Ghetto Nuovo, so that a funeral cortège will follow exactly the same route. It is traditional for the hearse to make a complete circle round the Ghetto Nuovo, as a symbol of farewell to this narrow strip of land.

THE MUSEUM OF JEWISH ART IN VENICE

The Museum of Jewish Art was opened in Venice in 1955, in the Campo de Ghetto Nuovo (at No. 2902/B), and it has received many generous donations since that time. The Museum was rearranged in 1986 during the first phase of a plan which aims to combine all three synagogues in the Ghetto Nuovo into a single museum area, when additional exhibition rooms will be opened to the public as well. The two rooms open at present contain a valuable collection of fabrics and silverwork, most of which originate from the five Scuole in the Ghetto. In addition, there is a small collection of *ketubbot* (marriage contracts) from Italy, and other liturgical objects from other countries, given to the museum by private individuals.

CATALOGUE OF THE EXHIBITS IN THE MUSEUM OF JEWISH ART

ROOM I

Case 1
177 Kiddush chalice. Silver. Venice, late 18th century.
180 Kiddush cup. Silver. Venice, 18th century.
272 Sabbath candlesticks. Silver. Venice, early 19th century.

Case 2
168 Oil lamp. Silver. Venice, 18th century.
262 Bessamim box (perfume). Silver. Austro-Hungary, 19th century.
260 Bessamim box. Silver. Berlin, circa 1860.
261 Bessamim box. Silver. Moscow, circa 1880.
65 Kiddush cup holder. Silver. Venice, early 19th century.

Case 3
203 and 206 Shofar (ram's horn) used at Rosh Hashanah (New Year) and Yom Kippur (fasting and expiation).

Room I. Interior. The first room contains ritual objects in silver and silver gilt, mostly manufactured in Venice.

Room I. Case 2. Box for bessamin (perfume), *Right* (261) Silver. Moscow, circa 1880. The synagogue is usually sprinkled with aromatic oils at the end of the Sabbath celebrations.

163

Case 4

163 Citron box. Silver and silver gilt. Venice, early 19th century.

179 Citron box. Silver. Venice, early 19th century.

Case 5

267 Hanukah lamp. Brass. Holland, 18th century.

298 Hanukah lamp. Silver. Neusöhl (Austria), circa 1750. Donated by Luigi Jarach.

Case 6

181 Hanukah lamp. Silver. Russia, 18th century. Donated by Gino Cesana.

195 Hanukah lamp. Silver. Germany, 19th century. Donated by Gino Cesana.

193 Hanukah lamp. Silver. Neusöhl (Austria), circa 1750. Donated by Giorgio and Alix Levi.

193

Case 7

204 Pesach plate. Silver and precious stones. Venice, 19th century.

Case 8

200 Purim plate. Pewter. Germany, 18th century. Donated by Gino Cesana.

196 Case for the Book of Esther. Silver gilt. Middle East, 19th century. Donated by Gino Cesana.

307 The Book of Esther. Manuscript on parchment. Venice, 19th century.

Room I. Case 6. Hanukah lamp. (195) Silver. Germany, 19th century.

Case 9

263 Shadai (amulet). Silver. Northern Italy, 19th century. Donated by Paolo Alazrachi.

304 Shadai. Silver. Piedmont, 18th century. Donated by E. Vitali.

198 Shadai. Silver. Venice, 19th century. Donated by Gino Cesana.

303 Shadai. Silver. Piedmont, 19th century. Donated by E. Vitali.

305 Shadai. Silver filigree. Venice, early 19th century. Donated by E. Vitali.

176 Shadai. Silver gilt. Venice, 19th century.

Room I. Case 8 (307) Meghilat Esther (Book of Esther) Manuscript on parchment. Venice, 19th century. (196). Case for the Book of Esther. Silver gilt. Middle East, 19th century.

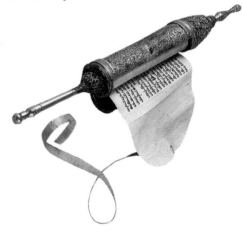

159 Binding for a prayer book. Silver and silver gilt. Venice, early 19th century. (Coats of arms of the Trieste and Vivante families.)

151 Shadai. Mother of pearl. Livorno, 19th century. Donated by P. Coen.

174 Shadai. Silver filigree and silver gilt. Venice, 18th century.

178 Binding for a prayer book. Silver. Venice, early 18th century.

302 Shadai. Silver filigree. Venice, early 19th century. Donated by E. Vitali.

Room I. Case 9. Shadai (174) Amulet for a cradle. Silver filigree and silver gilt. Venice, 18th century.

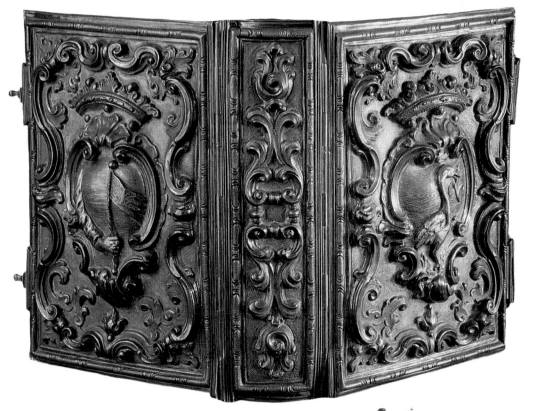

Room I. *Case 9*. Prayer book binding (*159*). In silver and silver gilt. Venice, early 19th century.

175 Binding for a prayer book. Silver gilt. Venice, 18th century.

Case 10

299 Menorah (lamp). Silvered bronze. Venice, 19th century. Donated by P. Sereni.

182 Offertory box. Silver. Moscow, 1888. Donated by L. Jarach.

End wall

Sefer Torah. Decoration for the Scroll of the Torah (the scroll itself is not displayed for religious reasons).

184 Atarah (crown). Silver gilt. Venice, 19th century.

169 Rimmonim (bell caps). Silver gilt. Venice, 19th century.

52T Meil (mantle). Velvet. Asti, 19th century. Donated by Artom-Sullam.

Room I. End wall, between the windows. Decorations for Scroll case: atarah (*184*), rimmonim (*169*), meil (*52T*).

Case 11

Yad (pointers shaped like little hands; used when reading the Torah).

140 Silver and silver gilt. Venice, 18th century.

141 Silver and silver gilt. Venice, 19th century.

Room I. Case 11. Two yads (pointers used when reading the Torah) *140* and *154*. Silver. Venice, 17th century.

142 Silver. Venice, 17th century.

143 Silver. Venice, 18th century.

152 Silver. Venice, late 18th century.

153 Silver and silver gilt. Venice, 18th century.

154 Silver. Venice, 17th century.

155 Silver. Venice, 18th century.

197 Silver. Germany, 19th century. Donated by G. Cesana.

Keys to the Ark of the Covenant

144 Silver. Venice, 19th century.
146 Silver. Venice, 18th century.
145 Silver. Venice, 19th century.

Case 12

Tas (ornamental silver shield hung on the Torah Scroll)
166 Silver. Venice, 19th century.
95 Silver. Venice, 18th century.

95

187

199

160 Silver. Venice, 18th century.
93 Silver. Venice, 18th century.
187 Silver. Venice, 19th century.
199 Silver. Amsterdam, circa 1780.
   Donated by G. Cesana.
94 Silver. Venice, 18th century.

Room I. Case 14. Rimmonim (*165*). Pinnacles to decorate the top of the Scrolls. Silver. Venice, early 18th century.

Case 13

172 Rimmonim. Silver and silver gilt. Venice, 18th century.

Case 14

173 Rimmonim. Silver and silver gilt. Venice, 18th century.
165 Rimmonim. Silver. Venice, early 18th century.

Case 15

294 Rimmonim. Silver. Venice, 19th century.
296 Rimmonim. Silver. Origin unknown, 18th century.

Room I. Case 15. Rimmonim (*296*). Pinnacles to decorate the top of the Scrolls. Silver. Venice, 18th century.

Room I. Case 15. Rimmonim (*158*). Pinnacles to decorate the top of the Scrolls. Silver and polychrome enamel. Turkey, 17th century.

158 Rimmonim. Silver and polychrome enamel. Turkey, 17th century.

Case 16

185 Jug. Silver. Venice, 18th century.
85 *and* 86 Jug and washbasin. Bronze. Venice, 17th century.

In the four cylindrical cases

161 Rimmonim. Silver and silver gilt. Venice, 18th century.
139 Atarah. Silver and silver gilt. Venice, 18th century.

Room I. *Case 16.* Silver jug. Venice, 18th century (*185*). For washing the hands of the *Kohanim* (priests).

191 Rimmonim. Silver. Venice (?), 18th century (?)

189 Atarah. Silver and silver gilt. Venice, 18th century.

150 Atarah. Silver. Venice, 18th century.

19 Rimmonim. Silver. Origin unknown, 19th century.

148 Atarah. Silver. Venice, 17th century.

ROOM II

Case along the stairs

22 Hanukah lamp. Silver. Venice, early 18th century.

23 Hanukah lamp. Silver. Venice, early 19th century.

137 Atarah. Silver. Venice, 18th century.

300 Pidyon dish. Silver. Asti, 19th century. Donated by Artom-Sullam.

147 Atarah. Silver. Venice, 18th century.

64 Sabbath lamp. Silver. Venice, 19th century.

301 Sabbath lamp. Brass. Persia, 19th century.

219 Hanukah lamp. Bronze. Venice, 19th century.

215 Hanukah lamp. Bronze. Venice, 19th century.

138 Atarah. Silver. Venice, 18th century.

43, 44, 45, 47, 54, 60 Oil lamps. Silver. Venice, 19th century.

Wall to the right of stairs

254 Ketubah (marriage contract). Ruben Pesaro and Ester Sforni. Manuscript on parchment, tempera. Mantua? 1792.

255 Ketubah. Davide Luria and Speranza Sforni. Manuscript on parchment, tempera. Origin unknown, 1817.

253 Ketubah. Elia Vivante and Fanny Sforni. Manuscript on parchment, tempera. Mantua, 1837.

252 Ketubah. Abramo Dina and Ester Sinigaglia. Manuscript on parchment, tempera. Lugo, 1775.

257 Ketubah. Giacobbe Sinigaglia and Dolce Sinigaglia. Manuscript on parchment, tempera. Lugo, 1784.

254

252

To give some idea of the typical marriage contract, the following is a translation of Ketubah 252:

On the sixth day of the week, the eleventh of Sivan, of the year 5535 after the creation of the world, according to our calendar, here in Lugo, between the rivers Senio and Santerno and near the waters of a well, young Avraham has come forth (may God preserve his Rock), son of the late Ytzhak Dina (blessed be his memory) and has said to the chaste young Ester (may she be blessed amongst virgins) daughter of Mordechai Sinigaglia (may God preserve his Rock): 'Be my wife according to the laws of Moses and of Israel, and I shall revere thee, care for thee, feed thee as Jewish men revere, care for and feed their wives according to the law, and I shall give you as a dowry for your maidenhead two hundred silver zuzims as is your due, and your food, and your clothes, and whatever you need and more, according to the custom of the land'. And this maid Ester accepted, may she be blessed among women, and became the wife of our Avraham, may God preserve him on his Rock.

And this was the dowry she brought with her: twenty pieces of silver, and our Avraham accepted them, may God preserve him on his Rock, and he added twenty pieces of silver from his own purse, in addition to the two hundred zuzims that were her due.

And thus spake our bridegroom Avraham (may God preserve him on his Rock): 'This ketubah guarantees that the dowry and additional monies are accepted by me in return for the best part of all riches and goods possessed by me on this earth, goods that are mine already and goods that I shall acquire in the future; mortgaged and unmortgaged, all will be guaranteed as security against the repayment of the ketubah, dowry and additional monies, until they exist no longer, down to the very coat on my back, in life and in death, from this day forth for ever more.'

And so this bridegroom Avraham (may God preserve him on his Rock) has assumed responsibility for the ketubah, the dowry and additional monies, as responsibility must be assumed for all ketubot, dowries and additional monies, in respect of all the daughters of Israel, pure and chaste virgins, irrespective of any let or hindrance found in other documents. We, the undersigned witnesses, testify to this assumption of responsibility on behalf of our dear Avraham (may God preserve him on his Rock), in the presence of the aforenamed young, chaste lady Ester his wife, may she be blessed among women, by means of an object suitable for the ratification of this acceptance.

Pronounced valid and in order:
1st witness.
2nd witness.

(not on display) Decorations for scroll case: detail. with atarah and rimmonim.

Wall in front of stairs

219 Tik (cylindrical case for the Torah). Gilded wood. Venice, 18th century.

Aaron Hakodesh – Ark of the Covenant, Ceneda, 17th century, with eternal lamp (*ner tamid*) and curtain (*parokhet*).

Inside: dressings for two Torahs

28 Atarah. Silver. Venice, 18th century.

190 Rimmonim. Silver. Venice, 18th century.

54T Meil. Silk damask. France, circa 1715.

92 Tas. Silver. Venice, 19th century.

136 Atarah. Silver. Venice, 1771.

295 Rimmonim. Silver. Venice, 19th century.

3T Meil. Silk velvet. Venice, 18th century.

91 Tas. Silver. Venice, 19th century.

Large wall with sliding panels

31 Meil. Satin, with one plain and three brocade ties, silver, gold and multicoloured silk. Venice, 1770–80.

33 Parokhet. Wild silk, brocaded with silver and multicoloured silk. Venice, circa 1765–70.

17 Parokhet. Silk taffeta, bordered with multicoloured silk brocade. Italy (Venice?), 1775–80.

28 Cloth for covering the Torah. Silk taffeta, bordered and lined, brocaded with multicoloured silk and spun gold. Handmade lace of silver gilt. Venice, *c.*1745–50.

36 Meil. Crimson cut silk velvet, cut close at the edge and embroidered with silver and gold. Lyons (France), 1740–50.

18 Parokhet. Corded silk grosgrain, with spooled silk border, brocaded with multicoloured silk and chenille. Venice, 1760–65.

21 Parokhet. Red wool, with a herringbone border, patchworked with yellow cut silk velvet. Venice, second half of the 16th century.

14 Parokhet. High pile velvet, plain, backed with satin. Genoa, 17th–18th century.

7 Vestment. High pile silk velvet, hammered and brocaded, heightened with spun and filigree silver thread of various thicknesses. Italy (Venice?), first quarter of the 19th century.

The Jewish Museum possesses a rich collection of fabrics, manufactured in Italy and in France. About fifty examples of these are on display on mobile panels in Room II.

(not on display) Miniature bible. Parchment manuscript by 'Daniel son of the doctor Samuel son of Daniel Dajan'. Pisa, 1398 – Perugia 1405.

4 Parokhet. Spooled silk grosgrain, brocaded with multicoloured silk and silver. Lyons (France), *c*.1735.

3 Parokhet. Satin, embroidered with multicoloured silk. Venice, 18th–19th century.

22 Parokhet. Silk damask, hammered and brocaded with silver gilt lamé, spun and curled. France, 17th–18th century.

Upper border: Silk damask lamé, brocaded with gold and silver. France, 17th–18th century.

35 Vestment. Crimson cut silk velvet, embroidered with gold and silver. Italy (Venice?), 17th–18th century.

5 Parokhet. Silk damask, hammered and brocaded with multicoloured silk and filigree silver. Venice, first quarter of the 18th century.

6 Parokhet. Bordered silk grosgrain, brocaded with silver and multicoloured silk in diagonal stripes. Venice, 1755–60.

16 Parokhet. Border: High pile silk velvet. France, last quarter of the 17th century.

Centre: High pile silk velvet, double weave with a diagonal weft, backed with silver. Genoa, third quarter of the 18th century.

23 Meil. Silk taffeta with a tucked warp, embroidered with silver. Venice, early 18th century.

Parokhet. Curtain for the Ark of the Covenant, donated by the Levantine Community in 1804. It shows the Jews camping in the desert with rows of tents, manna, quails and the hand of Moses drawing water from the rock. Satin, embroidered with coloured silks.

11 Meil. Satin, embroidered with multicoloured silk and silver. Venice, 18th–19th century.

29 Parokhet. Spooled silk grosgrain, brocaded with multicoloured silk. Venice, circa 1760.

26 Parokhet. Silk pekin. France, 1780–90.

2 Parokhet. Satin, embroidered with multicoloured silk, silver and baroque pearls. Italy, second half of the 17th century.

34 Parokhet. Silk lampas (a kind of crepe). Lyons (France), 17th–18th century.

Front wall with sliding panels

30 Cloth for covering the Torah. Taffeta, with a loose thread design, embroidered with multicoloured silk and silver. Venice, late 18th century. Silver gilt, handmade lace border, 18th century.

32 Parokhet. Silk grosgrain, bordered, brocaded with multicoloured silk. Tours (France), 1740–60.

10 Parokhet. Grosgrain, embroidered with multicoloured silk. Italy, circa 1730.

24 Cloth. Linen gauze, embroidered with multicoloured silk. Italy, mid-17th century.

8 Vestment. Satin, embroidered with multicoloured silk. Jewish, mid-18th century.

19 Mappah. Cut silk velvet, plain, embroidered with silver. Venice, last quarter of the 18th century.

15 Parokhet. Border: Cut silk moquette. Venice, 16th–17th century.

Centre: High pile or embossed silk velvet. Venice, mid-18th century.

27 Parokhet. White cotton canvas embroidered with silver (originally silver gilt), and silver sequins. Venice, 16th–17th century.

Border: Green cut silk velvet, embroidered with silver. Venice (?), 19th century.

1 Parokhet. Silk taffeta, bordered, brocaded in multicoloured silk. Venice, circa 1765.

Cases in far wall
Right-hand side
43F Meil. Linen. Italy, 17th century.
44F Meil. Linen. Italy, 16th century.
48F Meil. Silk taffeta. Italy, 1760–65.
49F Meil. Silk grosgrain from Tours. France, 1750–55.
50F Meil. Satin brocade. Italy, 1800–1820.
75T Tallit purse. Silk velvet and gold. Venice, 19th century. Donated by the Artom-Sullam family.
112T Tallit (prayer shawl). Embroidered silk serge. Venice, 19th century. Donated by R. Jarach.

In the centre
2T Meil. Silk lampas. Venice, 17th century.
53T Meil. Velvet. Italy, 19th century.
70T Meil. Silk damask brocade. Venice, 18th century.
72T Meil. Embossed velvet. Venice, 19th century.

76T Meil. Satin. Venice, 18th century.

Left-hand side
31F Meil. Satin. Venice, 1770–80.
42F Meil. Brocaded silk taffeta. France, 18th century.
45F Meil. Silk grosgrain embroidered with silver. Italy, 16th–17th century.
46F Meil. Dupioni silk taffeta. Italy or France, 18th century.
47F Meil. Satin, embroidered in silver. Venice, 18th–19th century.

11T Tallit purse. Silk lampas ('ganzo'). Venice, 18th century. Donated by the Artom-Sullam family.
77T Tallit purse. Silk velvet and silver. Asti(?), 19th century. Donated by the Artom-Sullam family.
110T Tallit. Silk seersucker. Venice, 19th century. Donated by the Artom-Sullam family.
111T Tallit. Silk grosgrain. Asti (?), 19th century. Donated by the Artom-Sullam family.

GLOSSARY OF THE MOST IMPORTANT HEBREW WORDS IN THE TEXT

ALMEMAR see *bimah*.

AARON HAKODESH Ark of the Covenant. Cupboard in which the Scrolls of the Torah are kept. Built into the wall of the synagogue, facing towards Jerusalem. The doors of the cupboard are screened by a curtain.

ASHKENAZI A Jew from Germany, or from Central Europe. The Ashkenazi Jews speak or spoke Yiddish and as a result they have a particular way of pronouncing Hebrew, still the language of the liturgy.

ATARAH Crown, usually made of silver, found in the synagogue above the Scrolls of the Torah. Symbol of the supremacy of Divine Law.

BETH HA KNESSET Assembly hall, thus synagogue. Also called 'shool', or 'schule'. A room where meetings are held, and also for prayers and study.

BIMAH From the Greek *bema*, platform. Also called a *teve* (box), or *almemar*, from the Arabic *al mimbar*. Dais from which readings of the Torah are given, prayers said and blessings given.

HANUKAH Literally, 'inauguration'. This is the feast during which the nine-armed candlestick is lit. It celebrates the resistance of the Hebrew tribe of the Maccabees against the Syrians. It commemorates in particular the reconsecration of the Temple of Jerusalem in 164 BC after it had been profaned by Antioch IV of Syria. According to Talmudic legend, the small quantity of oil found in the Temple was miraculously enough to keep the lamps alight for eight days.

The ninth arm of the candlestick is called the 'shammas', the servant.

KETUBAH The marriage contract, which is written in Aramaic and based on an ancient text.

KIDDUSH Ceremony of blessing the Sabbath and other feast days with a carafe of wine.

KIPPUR A day of expiation of sins, spent in prayer and fasting.

KOSHER Term used to describe objects, and particularly foods, which are pure, either naturally or after preparation.

MAPPAH Lectern cloth for *bimah*

MEIL Ornamental cloth used to wrap the Scroll of the Torah.

MENORAH Lamp. Usually indicates the seven-armed candelabra in the Sanctuary in Jerusalem. It is held to be the oldest symbol of the Jewish people. The number seven records the seven days of the creation of the world.

MIDRASH School, mainly devoted to the study of the Scriptures. Literally 'research'.

NER TAMID Eternal flame which burns before the Ark.

PARNASSIM The superintendents of the synagogue.

PAROKHET Ornamental curtain covering the doors of the Ark. It is usually richly decorated with traditional designs. The Ark in the Temple of Jerusalem was hidden by such a curtain.

PESACH Literally 'passage', passover. It commemorates the

liberation of the Jews from slavery in Egypt. During the first two evenings of this celebration, the Haggadah, the Jewish passover story, is read.

PURIM Literally 'deliverance'. Feast recalling the salvation of the Persian Jews from annihilation. The Book of Esther, who was the Jewish wife of King Ahasuerus, is read; Esther succeeded in averting the danger. It has become a sort of Jewish Carnival, during which people don masks and perform plays.

RIMMONIM Two bell caps, usually made of silver, which decorate the Scrolls of the Torah, at the top of the Atarah. Literally 'pomegranates', probably because of their original shape.

ROSH HASHANAH New Year.

SABBATH Saturday, the day of prayer and rest, when all work is forbidden.

SEFER TORAH The Torah written according to certain rules, by specialists, for liturgical use. It is rolled around two highly decorated wooden staves.

SEPHARDIC JEWS Name used to designate Jews of Iberian origin and their descendants, spread all over the Mediterranean, and beyond. They spoke Ladino, also called Judeo-Spanish.

SHADAI Literally 'omnipotent'. Amulet hung over the cradles of newborn babies.

SHOFAR Ram's horn. Sounded at certain particular times, and at dramatic moments in order to invoke divine protection over the populace.

SIMHAT TORAH Literally 'the joy of the Torah'. The day when the Pentateuch is read in its entirety. On this day each synagogue will display all the Torahs in its possession.

SUKKOT Festival of Huts. Recalls the forty years spent wandering in the desert before the Jews gained the Promised Land. It is linked with ancient harvest festivals.

TALLIT Prayer shawl worn by men during morning devotions.

TAS Small seal, often made of silver, hung on the Scroll of the Torah as an ornament.

TIK Carved wooden container for the Torah, often very highly decorated. Used by the Sephardim.

TORAH Literally 'teaching', 'doctrine', but often translated as 'law'. The term is used to designate the Pentateuch, the five books of the Bible attributed to Moses (Genesis, Exodus, Leviticus, Numbers, Deuteronomy).

YAD 'Hand'. Small pointer in silver, often with a hand at one end, used during the reading of the Torah.

YESHIVA Centre for advanced religious studies, and also prayer room.

BIBLIOGRAPHY

AA.VV., *Gli Ebrei e Venezia. Secoli XIV–XVIII*. Papers of the convention held in Venice (Fondazione Cini) 5–10 June, 1983. Ed. Comunità, Milan, 1987.

AA.VV., *Venezia restaurata 1966–1986*. Electa, Milan, 1986.

I. Adler. *La pratique musicale savante dans quelques communautés juives en Europe au XVIIe et XVIIIe siécle*. Paris, 1966.

E. Ashtor, 'Ebrei, cittadini di Venezia', in *Studi Veneziani*, Vol. XVII–XVIII, 1975–76.

E. Ashtor, 'Gli inizi della comunita ebraica a Venezia', in *Rassegna Mensile d'Israele*. No. 11–12, 1978.

E. Bassi, *Architettura del Sei e Settecento a Venezia*. ESI, Naples, 1962.

C. Boccato, *L'antico cimitero ebraico di San Nicolo di Lido a Venezia*. Published by the Centro storico ebraico di Venezia, 1980.

C. Boccato, 'Ordinanza contro il lusso e sul "suonatore del sabato" nel Ghetto di Venezia nel sec. XVII', in *RMI*, No. 6–7, 1979.

C. Boccato, 'Testimonianze ebraiche sulla peste del 1630 a Venezia', in *RMI*, No. 9–10, 1975.

R. Calimani, *Storia del Ghetto di Venezia*. Rusconi, Milan, 1985.

G. Carletto, *Il Ghetto veneziani nel '700 attraverso i catastici*. Carucci, Rome, 1981.

D. Carpi, *The Activity of the "Italian Synagogue" of Venice on Behalf of the Jewish Communities of Eretz–Israel During the Years 1576–1733*, Tel Aviv, 1978.

D. Cassuto, *Ricerche sulle cinque sinagoghe (Scuole) di Venezia*. Ministry for Foreign Affairs, Department of Cultural Relations, Jerusalem. The Jerusalem Publishing House Ltd., 1978.

D. Cassuto, 'The Scuola Grande Tedesca in the Venice Ghetto', in *Journal of Jewish Art*, 1977.

B. Cooperman, 'Venetian Policy Towards the Levantine Jews in its Broader Italian Context', in AA.VV., *Gli Ebrei e Venezia*, 1987, pp. 65 ff.

S. Della Pergola, 'Aspetti e problemi della demografia degli ebrei nell'epoca preindustriale', in AA.VV., *Gli Ebrei e Venezia*, 1987, pp. 201 ff.

R. Finlay, *La vita politica nella Venezia del Rinascimento*, Milan, 1982.

R. Finlay, 'The foundation of the Ghetto: Venice, the Jews and the war of the League of Cambray', in *Proceedings of the American Philosophical Society*, No. 126, 1982.

U. Fortis, *Ebrei e sinagoghe*. Storti, Venice. 1988.

U. Fortis, *Il Ghetto sulla Laguna*. Storti, Venice, 1988.

U. Fortis and P. Zolli, *La parlata giudeo-veneziana*. Carucci, Assisi, Rome, 1979.

U. Fortis (compiled by), *Venezia Ebraica*. Carucci, Rome, 1979.

G. Gianighian and P. Pavanini (compiled by), *Dietro i palazzi. Tre secoli di architettura minore a Venezia 1492–1803*. Arsenale, Venice, 1984.

P. Ginsborg, *Daniel Manin e la rivoluzione veneziana del 1848–1849*, Milan, 1978.

M. Goodblatt, *Jewish Life in Turkey in the Sixteenth Century as Reflected in the Legal Writings of Samuel de Medina*. New York, 1952.

P. Grendler, *L'Inquisizione Romana e l'editoria a Venezia (1540–1605)*. Rome, 1983.

A. C. Harris, *La demografia del Ghetto in Italia (1516–1797)*, Rome, 1967.

D. Jacoby, 'Les Juifs à Venise du XIVe au milieu du XVIe siécle', in *Venezia centro di mediazione tra oriente e occidente (secoli XV–XVI) – Aspetti e problemi*, Firenze, 1977.

P. C. Ioly Zorattini, 'Gli ebrei a Venezia, Padova e Verona', in *Storia della cultura veneta*, Vicenza, 1980.

P. C. Ioly Zorattini, 'Gli ebrei nel Veneto dal secondo Cinquecento a tutto il Seicento', in *Storia della cultura veneta*, 4/II, Vicenza, 1984.

P. C. Ioly Zorattini, 'Gli ebrei nel Veneto durante il Settecento', in *Storia della cultura veneta*, 5/II, Vicenza, 1986.

F. C. Lane, *I mercanti di Venezia*, Turin, 1982.

F. C. Lane, *Storia di Venezia*, Turin, 1978.

G. Luzzatto, 'Sulla condizione economica degli ebrei veneziani nel secolo XVIII', in *RMI*, written in honour of Riccardo Bachi, No. 16, 1950.

G. Luzzatto, 'Norme suntuarie riguardanti gli ebrei – 27 febbraio 1697', in *Archivo veneto*, a. XVII, 1687.

D. J. Malkiel, 'A Separate Republic: the Mechanics and Dynamics of Venetian Jewish Self-Government 1607–1624', unpublished PhD thesis, Harvard 1988.

A . Milan, *Il Ghetto di Rome: illustrazioni storiche.* Rome, 1964.

B. Nunes Vais Arbib, 'La comunita israelitica di Venezia durante il Risorgimento', in *RMI*, No. 5–8, 1961.

A. Ottolenghi, *Il Governo democratico di Venezia e l'abolizione del Ghetto*, in R.M.I., V, 1930, pp. 88–104.

A. Ottolenghi, *Per il IV centenario della Scuola Canton. Notizie storiche sui templi veneziani di rito tedesco e su alcuni templi privati con cenni della vita ebraica nei secoli XVI–XIX.* Printed by the Gazzettino Illustrato, Venice, 1932.

R. Pacifici, *Le iscrizioni dell'antico cimitero ebraico a Venezia.* I. Palombo, Alexandria, 1937.

T. Pignatti (compiled by), *Le Scuole di Venezia.* Electa, Milan, 1981.

J. Pinkerfeld, *Le sinagoghe d'Italia.* Goldberg's Press, Jerusalem, 1954.

P. Preto, *Peste e societa a Venezia, 1576*, Vicenza, 1978.

B. Pullan, *Rich and Poor in Renaissance Venice. The Social Institutions of a Catholic State to 1620.* Harvard University Press, Cambridge MA, 1971.

B. Pullan, *La politica sociale dell Repubblica di Venezia 1500–1620.* II, Il Veltro, Rome, 1982.

B. Pullan, *The Jews of Europe and the Inquisition of Venice 1550–1670.* Barnes and Noble Books, Totowa NJ, 1983.

B. Pullan, *Gli ebrei d'Europa e l'Inquisizione a Venezia dal 1550 al 1670.* Il Veltro, Rome, 1985.

B. Ravid, *The Establishment of the Ghetto Vecchio in Venice, 1541.* In '*Proceedings of the 6th World Congress of Jewish Studies*'. II, Jerusalem, 1975, pp. 153–167.

B. Ravid, *Economics and Toleration in Seventeenth-Century Venice.* Jerusalem, 1978.

B. Ravid, 'The first charter of the Jewish merchants of Venice, 1589', in *A.J.S. Review*, No. 1, 1976.

B. Ravid, 'The Jewish mercantile settlement of 12th and 13th century Venice: reality or conjecture?', in *A.J.S. Review*, No. 2, 1977.

B. Ravid, 'The Religious, Economic and Social Background and Context of the Establishment of the Ghetti of Venice', in AA.VV., *Gli Ebrei e Venezia*, 1987, pp. 211 ff.

G. Reinisch Sullam, *Il Ghetto di Venezia, le sinagoghe e il museo.* Carucci, Rome, 1985.

G. Reinish Sullam. *Tesori d'arte ebraica a Venezia*, Venice, n.d.

C. Roth, *Gli Ebrei in Venezia.* Cremonese, Rome, 1933.

C. Roth, 'I Marrani a Venezia', in *RMI*, No. 5–6, 1933.

C. Roth, 'L'Accademia musicale del Ghetto veneziano', in *RMI*, No. 4, 1928.

M. G. Sandri and P. Alazraki, *Arte e vita ebraica a Venezia 1516–1797.* Sansoni, Florence, 1971.

S. Simonsohn (Ed.) *Responsa of R. Juda Arye Modena.* Jerusalem, 1956/7.

J. Starr, Romania. *The Jewries of the Levant after the Fourth Crusade.* Paris, 1949.

G. Tabacco, 'Andrea Tron e la crisi dell'aristocrazia senatoria a Venezia', *Udine*, 1980 (II ed.).

N. E. Vanzan Marchini, 'Medici ebrei e assistenza cristiana nella Venezia del '500', in *RMI*, No. 4–5, 1979.

Y. H. Yerushalmi, *From Spanish Court to Italian Ghetto. Isaac Cardoso: A Study in Seventeenth-Century Marranism and Jewish Apologetics.* Columbia University Press, New York, 1971.

172

KEY TO MAP

1 Scuola Grande Tedesca/
   Museum of Hebrew Art
2 Scuola Canton
3 Scuola Italiana
4 Scuola Spagnola
5 Scuola Levantina
6 Scuola Luzzatto
7 Scuola Luzzatto
   (current position)
8 Casa di riposo israelitica

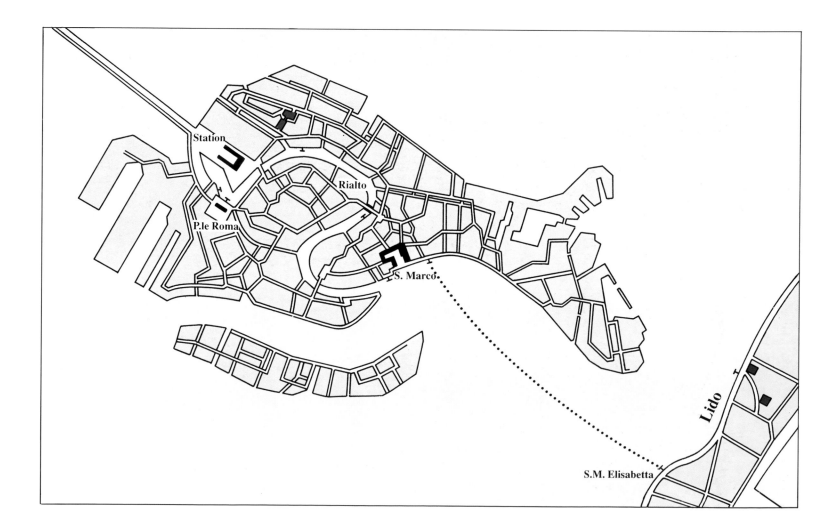

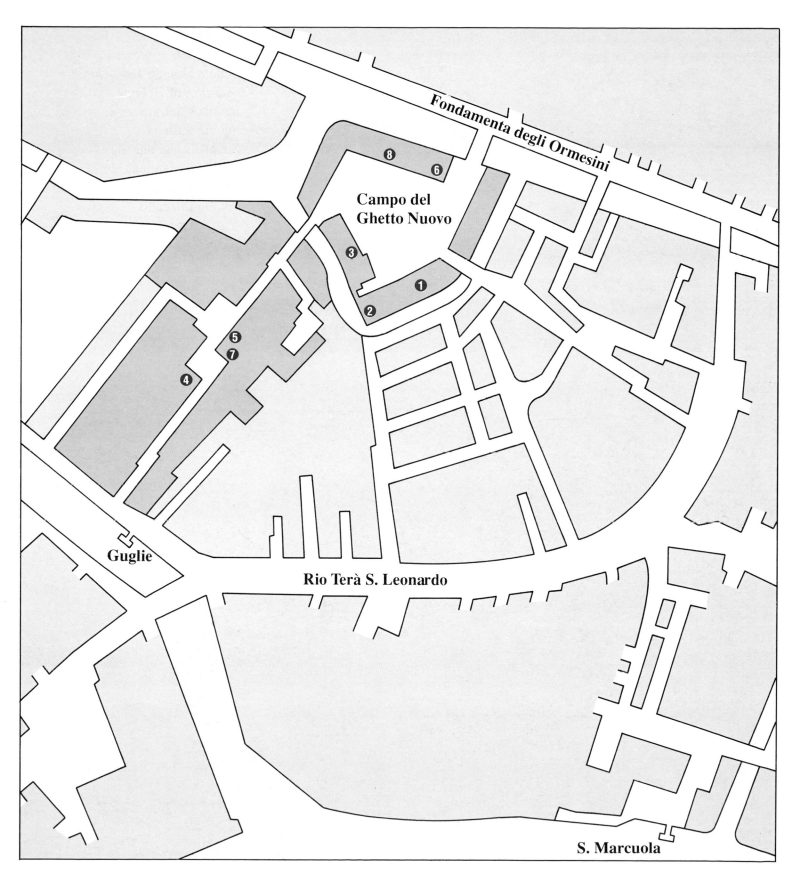

Fondamenta degli Ormesini

Campo del
Ghetto Nuovo

Guglie

Rio Terà S. Leonardo

S. Marcuola

INDEX

(Figures in *italics* refer to captions)